Praise for *The Boy Who Knew Too Much*

"Byrd's memoir almost reads like a suspenseful novel, and readers are sure to be gripped by the possible explanations she provides for (her son's) seemingly inexplicable memories. She also thoughtfully reflects on her own spirituality, and the ways in which her son's revelations challenged her Christian faith . . . On the whole, this is an affecting portrayal of parenthood, and an affectionate love letter from a mother to her unusual child. An eclectic mix of mystery, memoir, and the supernatural."

— Kirkus Reviews

"This is a wonderful book, intelligent, humorous, and overflowing with spiritual insights. One of the most transformative and thought-provoking books I've ever encountered."

— Jack Canfield, co-creator of the New York Times
#1 best-selling series Chicken Soup for the Soul®

"A riveting tale of a talented young boy with a love of the game and the natural talent to go along with it. More importantly, it is a story of how a mother's love can defy all logic and move mountains. Cathy Byrd is one heck of a baseball mom and a true advocate for all children."

— Tommy Lasorda, National Baseball Hall of Fame Dodgers manager

"A mother and son's extraordinary story demonstrates how our connections with loved ones do not end with the death of the physical body. Love's eternal bond brings our souls together again and again, leading to a richer sense of purpose in our lives."

— Eben Alexander, M.D., neurosurgeon, New York Times #1
best-selling author of Proof of Heaven

"This engaging, soulful, and highly entertaining memoir has the power to transform the way you think about life and death."

— John Gray, Ph.D., New York Times #1 best-selling relationship
author of all time, author of Beyond Mars and Venus

"In her inspirational new book, Cathy Byrd documents the compelling past-life memories of her young son. She also describes her own past-life regression recollections, linking both mother and son in a previous lifetime. The Boy Who Knew Too Much is an exciting journey into the mystery and power of past-life memories. I highly recommend this book."

— Brian L. Weiss, M.D., New York Times best-selling author of Many Lives, Many Masters

"Growing up in the 1970s, I've always viewed the Lou Gehrig story as somewhat mystical, from the famous farewell speech to my all-time favorite movie, The Pride of the Yankees. After reading the amazing journey of Cathy Byrd and Christian Haupt, the spirit of Gehrig resonates for the next generation of baseball fans to appreciate."

— Mark Langill, team historian, Los Angeles Dodgers

"The story you're about to read is at once, astounding, riveting, and truly unbelievable, yet before too long, as humanity continues waking up from its deep spiritual sleep, this story will be most believable. The nature of our soul and its adventure is eternal, yet we've

hidden this from ourselves for too long. For the courage of Cathy Byrd and her family, we can have a front-row seat on the revelations of a child who can see through the veils of time and space. The Boy Who Knew Too Much *is about to blow your mind. Enjoy!"*

— MIKE DOOLEY, NEW YORK TIMES #1 BEST-SELLING AUTHOR OF INFINITE POSSIBILITIES

"A testimonial to the fact that children can be our greatest teachers when it comes to spirituality and matters of the heart. So many children are providing evidence that we are all infinite spiritual beings having a temporary human experience. A message of light and love that will appeal to baseball fans and non-baseball fans alike."

— DR. SHEFALI TSABARY, CLINICAL PSYCHOLOGIST, NEW YORK TIMES BEST-SELLING AUTHOR OF THE CONSCIOUS PARENT

"This compelling, trustworthy book is a most reassuring guide for those whose children share vivid recollections of their previous lives, and anyone who is curious to learn more about this widely documented field of scientific study."

— MICHAEL BERNARD BECKWITH, FOUNDER OF AGAPE INTERNATIONAL SPIRITUAL CENTER AND AUTHOR OF SPIRITUAL LIBERATION

"The Boy Who Knew Too Much is a real-life story about a young boy, a talent for baseball, and a memory of a past life. It poses the most important question you can ask: do I only live once? One game, nine innings, and out forever! Or do I live many lives? Beautifully written, with integrity and humor, this gripping story might change the way you choose to play this game called life."

— ROBERT HOLDEN, PH.D., HAPPINESS EXPERT, BEST-SELLING AUTHOR OF SHIFT HAPPENS!

"Experience this joyful journey of knowingness. This story will remind you of your own eternal soul, and how we timeless beings share this earthly existence with others to learn and experience the connected force of love."

— JAMES VAN PRAAGH, SPIRITUAL MEDIUM, TEACHER, AND AUTHOR OF THE POWER OF LOVE

"For her debut publishing venture, Cathy Byrd offers a memoir of exceptional intrigue that at times reads like the pursuit of The Da Vinci Code. *Told with the skills of both investigator and spiritual pilgrim, it is also a tale of the connection between mother and child beyond the unexpected—a love story of the spirits."*

—ELLIOT MINTZ, RENOWNED MEDIA CONSULTANT

"Meeting Christian and Cathy Byrd and doing a past-life regression with them both allowed me to witness for myself the extraordinary life story of Lou Gehrig and Mom Gehrig. I fell in love with Christian and Cathy, and you will too as you dive into this riveting account of their adventure exploring reincarnation and the deeper truth that love always brings us together life after life. As a result of our work, Christian no longer has asthma and Cathy is fulfilling her soul's purpose in opening people's minds to the truth of our eternal existence. After I left their home, I immediately called my friend Dr. Wayne Dyer, and with awe and contagious enthusiasm I shared their story with him. I know that as soon as you turn the last page of this exceptional book, you too will be passionately sharing Christian's and Lou Gehrig's story with everyone and carrying the light of their soul in your heart."

— MIRA KELLEY, REGRESSIONIST, BEST-SELLING AUTHOR OF BEYOND PAST LIVES

THE BOY WHO KNEW TOO MUCH

THE BOY WHO KNEW TOO MUCH

An Astounding True Story of a Young Boy's Past-Life Memories

CATHY BYRD

HAY HOUSE, INC.
Carlsbad, California • New York City
London • Sydney • Johannesburg
Vancouver • New Delhi

Published and distributed in the United States by: Hay House, Inc.: www.hayhouse.com® • *Published and distributed in Australia by:* Hay House Australia Pty. Ltd.: www.hayhouse .com.au • *Published and distributed in the United Kingdom by:* Hay House UK, Ltd.: www .hayhouse.co.uk • *Published and distributed in the Republic of South Africa by:* Hay House SA (Pty), Ltd.: www.hayhouse.co.za • *Distributed in Canada by:* Raincoast Books: www.raincoast .com • *Published in India by:* Hay House Publishers India: www.hayhouse.co.in

Cover design: Tricia Breidenthal • *Interior design:* Pamela Homan
Credits for color insert photos: Photos on pages 1, 2, 4, 7–12, 14–15 courtesy of the author. Photo on page 1 by Karen Halbert Photography. Photos on pages 3, 11–12 courtesy of National Baseball Hall of Fame Library, Cooperstown, NY. Photos on pages 4–6 courtesy of Ed Lobenhofer. Photos on pages 6 and 13 by Jon SooHoo/Los Angeles Dodgers LLC. Photos on pages 8 and 12 by Charlotte Haupt. Photo on page 9 by Peter Lars © Cornerstone Photography. Photo on page 13 courtesy of Ken Hawkins. Photo on page 14 by © Ultimate Exposures, Inc. Photo on page 15 Courtesy of Lori Dickman. Photo on page 15 by Marc Belmonte. Photo on page 16 by Michael Coons.
End paper photo: by Bettmann Collection/Getty Images.
The article in Chapter 10, "Three-year-old a film star, pitching prodigy," is reprinted Courtesy Fox Sports West, www.foxsportswest.com.
Nike logo is a registered trademark of NIKE, Inc. Use or appearance of the Nike logo does not imply any affiliation with or endorsement by NIKE, Inc. • Los Angeles Dodgers logo use with permission by Los Angeles Dodgers LLC. • Wilson logo used with permission by Wilson Sporting Goods Co. • MLB logo is a registered trademark of Major League Baseball™ and is used with permission. • Majestic® logo used with permission by Majestic® and VFC.

Cataloging-in-Publication Data is on file at the Library of Congress

Hardcover ISBN: 978-1-4019-5342-3

13 12 11 10 9 8 7 6 5 4
1st edition, March 2017

Printed in the United States of America

SUSTAINABLE
FORESTRY
INITIATIVE
Certified Sourcing
www.sfiprogram.org
SFI-01268

SFI label applies to text stock only

To Charlotte and Christian.
May you always see life
as a daring adventure.

CONTENTS

FOREWORD

As an avid reader and the co-author of more than 150 books, I can honestly say that the book you hold in your hands is one of the most transformative and thought-provoking I've ever encountered. As the co-author of the Chicken Soup for the Soul® books, I receive countless requests to provide endorsements for books, and because I don't take these requests lightly, there are very few that I feel compelled to recommend. However, this extraordinary book not only hooked me from the start and kept me turning the pages until the very last word, I couldn't stop talking about it with everyone I met. You are about to embark on a remarkable journey that could very well change the way you view life and death forever.

At first blush Cathy Byrd's story may seem as improbable to you as it did to her. What makes this story so compelling is that Cathy Byrd is a Christian who previously never believed in reincarnation. As you follow her miraculous journey of a mother trying to make sense of the things her young son is telling her about his former life as a professional baseball player, you will be stretched to examine your own beliefs regarding life before life and after life on this planet. But beyond this, it will also inspire you to honor your intuition, listen to the children in your life, love without limits, and make the most of each day that you are blessed with. You see this book is really several books in one. In addition to being a book about reincarnation, it's also a book about learning to deeply listen to and trust our children, a book about baseball, and a book about how the universe constantly conspires to arrange events to expand our consciousness.

I've long believed we are all infinite spiritual beings having a temporary human experience on earth, and *The Boy Who Knew Too Much* is a powerful testimony to this grand idea. I was first introduced to the concept of a soul living more than one lifetime at 16 years of age. Growing up in a Christian home, this was all new to me, but somehow it rang true. When I was in graduate school at the University of Massachusetts, a professor gave me the book *Life After Life* by Dr. Raymond Moody and later *Life Before Life* by Dr. Helen Wambach, both of which deepened my belief in past lives. Since that time I have had several vivid past-life recall experiences, some arising spontaneously and others facilitated by psychologists. And I have also read numerous academic books on the subject.

So the story of Cathy and her son, Christian Haupt, did not surprise me, but I was completely mesmerized by it. I had never read such a long, beautifully written, deeply truthful and transparent account of the gradual revelation of a child's past-life memories and a skeptical mother's gradual acceptance of it. Because there are so many unexpected twists and turns along the way, I don't want to reveal any more details for fear of spoiling your own experience of the mysterious unfolding of it all.

What I can say is that I believe this story will touch you on many levels—as a parent, a spiritual seeker, and a fan of baseball. Lou Gehrig is one of the true legends in the history of baseball, and the story of his relationship with his mother and their relationship with Babe Ruth is totally fascinating. No matter how much you already know about their tumultuous relationship with Babe Ruth, you will learn more about their lives.

As a baseball fan who had lived in Los Angeles for more than ten years, I had always admired Tommy Lasorda, the former manager of the Los Angeles Dodgers, especially since the time Mark Victor Hansen and I co-authored *Chicken Soup for the Baseball Fan's Soul* with him, but in reading about how he quickly recognized Christian as a young baseball prodigy and befriended and supported him and his family in so many beautiful ways, I learned so much more about his sweet compassion and deep humanity.

I first had the good fortune to meet Cathy when she reached out to me by e-mail requesting a short endorsement quote for her book. After reading the book, I was more than willing to give her a glowing endorsement, which I did. But then a few weeks later she decided to sign up for a workshop I was conducting for a small group of people on Maui. Over the five days of the workshop we all fell in love with her—her passion, her enthusiasm, her love of life, her sense of humor, her authenticity and transparency, her thirst for learning, her dedication to her mission, her sincere support for each person in the workshop, and her seemingly boundless energy.

A week after returning from Maui, Cathy contacted me and asked if I would consider writing the foreword for the book. Originally, she thought Dr. Wayne Dyer would write the foreword, until fate intervened. Wayne had met Cathy and her son, Christian, at the Hay House Writer's Workshop in June 2015 in Maui, just two months prior to his passing. It turned out that Wayne was also passionate about the subject of children's past-life memories and therefore became a big supporter of the book you are about to read.

When Cathy met Wayne, he was putting the final touches on the last book he would ever write, *Memories of Heaven*—a compilation of stories about children from around the world who came here with memories of Heaven, memories that reinforce the idea that the soul never dies. Wayne and his co-author, Dee Garnes, had collected thousands upon thousands of personal anecdotes about young children reporting how they remembered choosing their parents for this journey, how they had invisible friends that only they could see, memories of past lives, visitations with God, and much more. The experiences described in *Memories of Heaven* provide clues to an infinite spiritual realm far greater than we can perceive with our five senses.

The father of eight children, Wayne had his own personal experience with a child who came into the world bearing past-life memories. As a toddler, his daughter Serena spoke in a foreign language, frequently spoke about her "other" family, and vividly described planes dropping bombs and wiping out her village. Hearing these odd things come out of his daughter's mouth is what convinced Wayne that we all come here with memories and experiences from our previous lives.

I believe it is no accident that Wayne's final piece of work, which was published after his passing, is about Heaven. Here are some of Wayne's thoughts on the subject of children's past-life memories in an excerpt of his writing from *Memories of Heaven*:

> *There is a growing body of evidence that is being subjected to rigid scientific examination procedures, which points to the fact of "life before life." This idea is now a verifiable conclusion by those who have studied*

this phenomenon in depth. I have long held that children are much more than just biological beings shaped by their genetic makeup and the environment in which they are immersed. They are essentially spiritual beings who bring with them wisdom and a host of experiences from having lived here in previous lifetimes.

Who we are is obviously not these bodies we inhabit . . . From all that we can gather from what our children tell us, our souls are indestructible and they transcend time and space in a way that remains mysterious to all of us.

I suggest that you begin to view any of the young children in your life as new arrivals from Heaven. Communicate with them by asking questions about their recollections. Above all, do not dismiss anything they might say, regardless of how absurd it may sound to you. Make an effort to engage your children in your conversation, and rather than perceiving yourself as their teacher, allow them to take on that role with you. Be inquisitive and an active listener by drawing them out and taking a genuine interest in whatever they might offer.

Be aware that little ones, who are imparting those mysterious words that you might find difficult to grasp, speak their own unique truth. Let their honesty and excitement about these "weird" memories from Heaven remind you that you too were once a small child, and that little child resides within you at all times.

— Dr. Wayne W. Dyer

As *The Boy Who Knew Too Much* teaches us, it is important to never brush off or doubt these remembrances that flow out of the mouths of young children, and to keep in mind the famous observation of Mark Twain: "It ain't what you don't know that gets you into trouble. It's what you know for sure that just ain't so."

That said, I think Mark Twain would have loved this book. I do, and I am confident you will too. As incredible as Cathy's story sometimes seems, it is all true; if you allow it, it has the potential to reawaken in you an appreciation of the magical mystery of life and what a grand adventure it is—full of things we may never fully understand and can only marvel and wonder at.

And now I invite you to sit back, relax, and enjoy Cathy's amazing and inspiring story.

— Jack Canfield
Co-creator of the #1 *New York Times* best-selling Chicken Soup for the Soul® series

INTRODUCTION

"Kids say the darndest things!" was the byline for *Art Linkletter's House Party*, a television show popular in the 1960s. Given that one of the gifts of childhood is a robust imagination, Art's show displayed a steady flow of insightful and often hilarious material over decades.

It can be easy to dismiss what comes out of the mouths of babes, but paying more thoughtful attention to those "darndest things" can sometimes reveal innocent wisdom under the surface. The fascinating story you are about to read is like many similar stories known personally to families around the world. Most have kept such stories private in order to avoid ridicule in our modern society. This story recounts the past-life memories of a young child, Christian Haupt, which invokes the surprising possibility that we live more than one lifetime here on earth. "Surprising," though, is a relative term, for many of the world's great faiths are open to the possibility of reincarnation.

As a neurosurgeon, I've spent my career studying the brain, mind, and consciousness. At age 54, I thought I was close to some understanding of their relationship with one another. That is, until November 2008, when my entire worldview was suddenly and unexpectedly thrown asunder after a weeklong coma due to severe bacterial meningitis, from which my doctors did not expect any chance of recovery.

Inexplicably, I was blessed with a full recovery over several months but found that I had to reconsider everything I thought I knew about the brain's relation to consciousness. I summarized my dilemma and its early resolution in the book *Proof of Heaven*, in which the extreme challenge of explaining the rich experience of my spiritual odyssey during coma could not be based on the physical workings of the brain alone. Over the years (as shared in my second book, *The Map of Heaven*), it has become clear that the entire scientific community is going through a similar challenge in understanding whether any facet of our awareness continues following the death of the physical body. Consciousness seems to be a primary substance of the universe that leads to the emergence of all of reality witnessed as the physical realm.

Of crucial importance in our scientific era is the fact that our emerging views of the nature of consciousness not only *allow* for the possibility of reincarnation, they actually *imply* that reincarnation offers the greatest explanatory potential for much of human experience. This is especially evident in some cases of child prodigies, including the subject of this book, Christian Haupt, who exhibited exceptional skills in baseball from a very early age. Reincarnation might also explain cases of exceptional genius, such as the prolific childhood composer Wolfgang Amadeus Mozart and the world-class mathematician Snrinivasa Ramanujan, among others.

Although some might summarily dismiss this as a story firmly entrenched in the "supernatural," our modern scientific investigations into the nature of consciousness, including past-life memories in children, suggest instead that it is simply *our understanding* of the *natural* world that is in need of revision. The natural order of things increasingly appears to be one in which consciousness is the "creator and governor" of this realm, as was so eloquently stated by Sir James Jeans in his musings over the mysterious facts emerging from experiments in quantum mechanics about the fundamental nature of reality.

Families are occasionally surprised or confused when young children, often just beginning to form words, begin talking about events that have nothing to do with their current reality. They report dreams of situations and scenes that seem quite foreign. Case studies reveal that specific events are spoken of or acted out in what may appear to be a game of pretense, but the child insists it is real. Some children declare they have different parents or live in another location, often with emotional intensity that cannot be ignored. While some parents dismiss such claims, others (like Christian's mother, Cathy) pay attention and search for explanations.

Courageous scientists at the University of Virginia (UVA) School of Medicine have been studying cases like Christian's since 1967 when Dr. Ian Stevenson, then chairman of Psychiatry at UVA, founded the Division of Perceptual Studies (DOPS) there. Over the past fifty years, the DOPS has investigated and documented over 2,500 cases of children who recall past lives. This work has recently been carried forward by Dr. Jim Tucker, Director of DOPS, who you'll see has been involved in the investigation of Christian's case.

Scientists who investigate such cases meticulously interview the child about specific details of their memories and look to validate such information through other sources. They generally focus on those cases in which the details of a previous life remembered by the child could not have been learned through any typical means, especially through parents and other family members. The ideal age range for uncovering such memories extends from two to six years. The younger the child, the better, in order to minimize the chance that the child could have acquired the information through other exposure. Generally, after age eight such memories have often faded away.

Such investigations tend to avoid those involving memories of *famous* persons because of the heightened possibility for fraud given the widespread availability of information on such persons from books and Internet sources. Scientists prefer more anonymous cases in which crucial verifiable information supporting the reality of reported connections could not possibly have come to the child through normal means. Thus, even in such cases involving famous persons, they seek the more obscure facts that one could generally not come to know through standard sources. Amazingly, many such obscure facts are revealed throughout the story portrayed in *The Boy Who Knew Too Much*.

A significant gift of this book, beyond the powerful demonstration of the reality of past-life memories in children, is its support for the notion that reincarnation is about evolution of the soul group, rather than just of individual souls—we tend to reincarnate with other members of our soul group, seemingly to continue our ongoing soul lessons. This follows from the central theme of so many near-death experiences and death-bed visions concerning the appearance of the souls of departed loved ones around the time of a soul's transition—that we are all in this together, and our connections with loved ones do not end with the death of the physical body. This bond of love is what brings us together again and again through various lifetimes.

Many will come to acknowledge the courage of Christian's mother, Cathy Byrd, for her generous public sharing of this deeply personal family story, at some potential risk to her own (and her children's) peace of mind due to the possibility of adverse responses. After all, we hold these kinds of beliefs close to our hearts, and finding them challenged arouses intense passions and reactions.

I suspect this book will have its most profound effect by providing permission for others to share similar experiences that suggest we are vastly greater than our physical bodies, and that our existence serves a purpose grander than we can currently imagine.

So, enjoy the extraordinary true story of young Christian Haupt and his mother, and the astonishing possibilities that it and similar stories imply for all of human existence. It opens the door to far more meaning and purpose in our lives, woven into a rich tapestry bound by loving connections!

— Eben Alexander, M.D., neurosurgeon and author of *Proof of Heaven* and *The Map of Heaven*

CHAPTER ONE

BASEBALL FEVER

"Our birth is but a sleep and a forgetting;
The Soul that rises with us, our life's Star,
Hath had elsewhere its setting
And cometh from afar."

WILLIAM WORDSWORTH

Anything can happen in baseball.

I've been a fan of the game for exactly 3.5 years as the result of our six-year-old son's uncanny affection for America's favorite pastime. A story shared by countless Little League moms since the proverbial first pitch, I'm sure. Every mother wants to believe that her child will be that one in a million who makes it to the big leagues, but this is not a story about that. This is the story of a young boy who opened our eyes to the rich history of baseball in the 1920s and '30s, and showed us all that what truly matters in this lifetime is the difference we make in the lives of others.

When our son, Christian Haupt, was five years old, we received a call from a representative of the Los Angeles Dodgers, requesting to come to our home and interview him about his baseball adventures. It may sound strange that a Major League Baseball team was interested in documenting the exploits of a boy who was barely old enough to play T-ball, but what was far more interesting than the five-minute documentary that aired on television is what our son had been telling us behind closed doors for the previous two years about having been a "tall baseball player" in another lifetime. This is the story we have shared only with our closest friends and family—until now.

The YouTube videos of our son, Christian, playing baseball had been viewed by over five million people by the time he reached his fifth birthday. However, our real journey began when the very first video we ever uploaded to YouTube happened to catch the eye of actor/comedian Adam Sandler. In a strange twist of fate, within days of uploading the YouTube video of our then two-year-old son hitting and throwing baseballs, we found ourselves on a plane to Boston to film Christian's baseball-playing cameo role in the movie *That's My Boy*. This serendipitous trip to Boston was a turning point for us in truly understanding the depth of our two-year-old son's passion for baseball.

Christian's love of the game began on the sidelines of his big sister, Charlotte's, T-ball games when he was still in diapers. When he caught his first glimpse of a real Little League game, he studied the eight- and nine-year-old players with laser-like focus and spent countless hours every day imitating their moves. It was quite amusing to see a toddler winding up for a pitch with a big leg kick, or twirling his bat and then pounding it on home plate before swinging with all his might. Christian was happy to put on a display for anyone who was willing to watch, and when he was in baseball mode he preferred for us to call him Baseball Konrad—an alter ego he had created for himself using his middle name, Konrad. For the most part, it was an endearing hobby that brought us great joy, but there were moments when our patience was pushed to the limit.

Since the time our son could walk, he carried a small, wooden baseball bat with him wherever he went. By the age of two, he insisted on wearing baseball pants, a baseball jersey, and baseball cleats every day—even in the heat of summer. Every time Christian saw a white line in the sky, he excitedly pointed to the sky and said, "Look, Mommy! A baseline!" He took a bite out of a tortilla chip and said, "It looks like home plate!" He once saw a white, rectangle-shaped napkin on a bathroom floor and proclaimed, "That's cool! A pitcher's mound." If life was a Rorschach test, Christian was seeing baseball.

My husband, Michael, and I had seen Charlotte go through a Disney princess phase as a toddler, but this was different. Our son, Christian, was different. He had no interest in toys or television, and rarely interacted with the other kids in our mommy-and-me classes, instead pulling me away to pitch balls to him on the playground while his classmates participated in normal two-year-old activities such as playing with bubbles and building block towers with their peers. Most disconcerting was the fact that our attempts to deter him from his singular focus on baseball just made him more insistent. Christian's constant pleas for us to pitch balls to him every minute of the day, both inside and outside of our house, was downright exhausting for both of us. Most days we would play baseball with him morning, noon, and night, yet he still begged for more. Not a day went by that baseball was not on his mind. We once attempted to get him out of his baseball jersey and into a button-down shirt for a family portrait with his cousins, and he cried so hard that eventually both his red eyes and his baseball jersey made it into the photo. Michael and I were concerned that his passion for baseball might be borderline obsessive.

In the summer of 2011, Michael took a temporary consulting job for Lockheed Martin that required him to travel to Dallas/Fort Worth on a weekly basis. My job as a residential real estate agent allowed me the flexibility to work from home and bring my kids to my appointments if necessary, but this balancing act became more challenging with Michael out of town five days a week. Before dragging my kids with me to show homes, I would spend two to three hours each morning playing baseball with them at the local Little League fields. Regardless of how much time we spent at the fields, the ending to each outing was always the same—me carrying Christian to the car under my arm like a football while he kicked and screamed for "one more." Following the struggle, he would inevitably collapse into a deep sleep within moments of being strapped into his car seat.

"Why do we keep doing this," Charlotte frequently asked, during the short ride back to our house, "when we know that he is going to cry every time we leave?"

She was right. *Why bother?* But it was Christian's undeniable passion when he was in the role of Baseball Konrad that kept me coming back for more.

Michael was in Dallas when my best friend of 15 years, Cinthia, invited us to be her guests at a Los Angeles Dodgers game. I doubt Michael would have chosen to join us even if he had been in town because he'd had a hard time adapting to Christian's love of baseball, primarily because Michael had been born and raised in Germany, where baseball is basically nonexistent. Despite being a Southern California native, this would be my first outing to Dodger

Stadium, or any Major League Baseball game, for that matter. Cinthia had established herself as a massage therapist to the stars in Los Angeles over the years, and her clients constantly gave her tickets to sporting matches, awards shows, and special events. From our late 20s to early 30s, Cinthia and I could be found at nearly every big sporting event, movie premiere, and concert in town. Although our social lives had slowed down considerably since then, the one thing that remained the same was that whenever we were together, fun seemed to follow us.

"Aunt Cinthia" had a knack for making Charlotte and Christian feel special. She had been at every significant event in their lives thus far, including their births and baptisms, so it was fitting she would be there for Christian's initiation to Dodger Stadium. Little did we know at the time that the 50-year-old stadium in the heart of downtown Los Angeles would become our home away from home in the years to come. The first thing Cinthia did when we arrived at Dodger Stadium was take us to the souvenir shop to buy gifts for Charlotte and Christian. Charlotte swooned over the stuffed animals while Christian proudly posed for pictures in his Dodger uniform next to the life-size Dodger mannequins. Cinthia then escorted us to the very exclusive Dodger Stadium Club, where we watched the game and ate lunch at a table overlooking the field. Christian was completely mesmerized by the action on the field, and barely moved for the duration of the game, something completely uncharacteristic of a kid who rarely sat still. I had never seen him quite so serious, or speechless, in all his life, but he was clearly enjoying the experience.

Following the game Cinthia talked our way into a private restaurant at Dodger Stadium called the Dugout

Club. While Cinthia treated Charlotte to a Shirley Temple, I found a vacant hallway where Christian could get out some energy by hitting foam balls with his brand-new 18-inch souvenir bat.

"Your little boy's got quite the natural form as a lefty," a kind man stopped to comment, handing Christian a game ball he had caught that day and pointing to the hallway behind us. "The Dodger players will be walking out of those doors behind you anytime now. I bet you can get one of them to sign that ball for you if you ask real nicely."

Sure enough, the athletes started filing out of the door one by one to make their way to the elevator. A good-natured Dodger player in his mid-20s, who we later found out was star outfielder Matt Kemp, stopped on his way out to give Christian a high five and sign the ball. This was undoubtedly the best day of Christian's life to date, and he was officially hooked.

Christian and I made a return trip to Dodger Stadium a couple of weeks later for a tour of the stadium on a day when there was no game taking place. The highlights for Christian were sitting on the bench in the dugout where he had seen the Dodger players sitting, and rolling around on the field's red dirt, which he had affectionately named "Dodger dirt." When the tour guide gave him permission to practice his hitting and pitching on the dirt track surrounding the field, Christian was overjoyed.

By now I was an expert at pitching the tiny foam balls, so I managed to pitch to him and shoot a few video clips at the same time. As Christian whacked ball after ball into the stands with his little wooden bat, our tour companions egged him on with their cheers. He then asked me to switch to the role of catcher so he could practice his pitching skills.

"He's shaking off the sign!" a woman from our tour group exclaimed.

"What do you mean, 'shaking off the sign'?" I asked.

"The way he shakes his head back and forth and up and down before throwing the ball is exactly what the Major League pitchers do."

She further explained that the catcher gives the pitcher a sign as to what pitch to throw, and then the pitcher says yes or no, depending on whether or not he is in agreement with the call.

"I wonder if the Dodgers would ever let a little kid throw a ceremonial first pitch at a game?" she said, pointing to the pitcher's mound. "That would sure be cute to see that little guy on that big mound."

Without knowing it, this knowledgeable woman had planted a seed in my mind.

When we arrived back at home, the wheels in my mind were spinning about the woman's suggestion to have Christian throw a ceremonial first pitch. I went to my computer and searched YouTube to see if a toddler had ever thrown a first pitch at a Major League Baseball game before. I was treated to videos of U.S. Presidents, Hollywood celebrities, and rap stars on the mound, but surprisingly, there were no young kids to be found among the ceremonial-first-pitch hurlers.

Even though YouTube had only been in existence for five years in 2011, it was already a household name, primarily due to Justin Bieber's historic rise to fame after being "discovered" on YouTube in 2009. I had no interest in having our two-year-old son follow in the footsteps of Justin Bieber, but I figured YouTube might be a good vehicle for getting the attention of whoever it was at the

Dodgers' executive office who was responsible for deciding who gets to throw a first pitch.

I knew our window of time was limited because the main thing that made Christian unique was his early development when it came to hitting and throwing a baseball. Similar to babies who reach milestones like walking or talking earlier than their peers, you can always count on the majority of kids to catch up over time. I had no doubt that the "cuteness" factor would be long gone by the time he was five years old and indistinguishable from any other Little League baseball player.

When Michael got back in town, I told him about my harebrained scheme to have Christian throw a first pitch, and successfully talked him into creating a one-minute montage of the video clips I had shot at Dodger Stadium so we could upload it to YouTube. YouTube was already flooded with videos from proud parents showcasing their children's every move, so in that regard, the video we uploaded was really nothing special. I wrote the following description under the video:

> *Our two-year-old son loves baseball and getting to play at Dodger Stadium was the highlight of his life thus far. He insists on wearing cleats, batting gloves, baseball pants and a jersey every day. Nobody in our family ever watched or played baseball so his fascination with the sport came as quite a surprise to us. He went to his first MLB game 3 weeks ago and was lucky enough to get a game ball signed by Matt Kemp. He made up the nickname "Baseball Konrad" for himself when he plays, but his real name is Christian. We have*

a crazy dream that he might be able to throw a ceremo-
nial first pitch at a Dodger game before he turns three!

I e-mailed the YouTube link to my entire e-mail data-base, asking them to share the video with their family and friends, hoping the Dodgers would take notice if it racked up a lot of views. In retrospect, my prideful exuberance probably came across as a bit overzealous, but because of the events that were about to unfold, I can't say that I would take it back if given the chance.

A few days after uploading the video to YouTube, my husband received an e-mail from a woman asking if the boy in the video was his son. She introduced herself as a fellow Horned Frog, a reference to the mascot from his alma mater, Texas Christian University. She said her company, Sports Studio, was desperately trying to locate the little boy in the video for a baseball-playing role in a movie with Adam Sandler.

Because I'd spent the majority of my 43 years on this planet living in Southern California, I had seen all kinds of scams devised to exploit people's dreams of becoming Hollywood stars. I was sure that we were about to be the victims of some kind of YouTube hoax aimed at overly proud parents. My first question to Michael when he called from Texas to tell me about the e-mail was, "Is she asking for money?" Despite my skepticism, Michael decided to give her a call to request more information. As it turned out, Sports Studio was a legitimate casting agency that used social media websites, like YouTube, to find real-life athletes for sports-specific roles in commercials, television shows, and films. Who knew this was a thing?

"The casting director wants you to send her a video of Christian catching a ball with a baseball glove by the end of the day," Michael said.

"Michael, you realize he has never done that before, right?"

"How hard can it be?"

Christian had been hitting and throwing balls for over a year, but we always rolled the balls back to him because we assumed he was still too young to catch with a glove. Our little boy was about to have a crash course in catching a baseball. By pure luck I happened to have a tiny glove for left-handed throwers because it was given to me by a girl-friend in a sports-themed gift basket when I was pregnant with Christian. Figuring that the odds of our son being a lefty were slim, I had tried to exchange the glove at three different sporting goods stores prior to his birth. Thankfully none of them had let me return it because, against all odds, Christian ended up being a lefty. Today this little glove would come in handy.

With Michael out of town, I needed a third person to play baseball with Christian so my hands would be free to shoot video clips with my handheld camera. My mom's boyfriend, Dennis, willingly obliged to meet us at the baseball field at 11 A.M. Dennis was in his element in any sports arena, being an all-around athlete and ex-jock himself.

"What if he can't catch?" he asked, when we arrived at the field.

"That's not an option," I said with a laugh.

Teaching a toddler to catch a baseball is hysterically funny to begin with, but two grown adults acting as if a child catching a ball was the greatest thing they had ever seen must have looked ludicrous. Luckily the only person in the vicinity to witness our shenanigans was the Little League groundskeeper, who was busy mowing the adjacent fields. Although Christian's catching skills were far from perfect, we were miraculously able to capture a few video clips where the ball actually landed in his glove. As we were getting some video clips of Christian hitting balls with a regular-size bat, the Little League groundskeeper turned off the engine on his large riding mower to watch what we were doing.

"The kid has talent," he yelled out to us. "Just make sure you keep it fun for him in the years to come."

We didn't bother explaining to him why we were taking our baseball video shoot so seriously, but I doubt he would have believed it anyway. I could hardly believe it myself until we boarded the plane to Boston, Massachusetts, two weeks later.

CHAPTER TWO

BABE RUTH WAS MEAN TO YOU?

"Grown men may learn from very little children, for the hearts of little children are pure, and, therefore, the Great Spirit may show to them many things which older people miss."

BLACK ELK, NATIVE AMERICAN SPIRITUAL LEADER

Our journey to Boston began with a bang when Christian, in terrible-two fashion, refused to let me fasten his seat belt. Witnessing my struggle to strap him into his seat, our gracious flight attendant came over to offer assistance. My son surprised us both when he loudly belted out, "When I was big, I didn't wear seat belts, and I drank alcohol." The flight attendant and surrounding passengers broke into laughter, while I did my best to wrangle my little despot into his seat.

"Someday you *will be* big," I said, as I held him down with one hand and secured the metal clip with the other, "but you *will always* wear a seat belt." I decided to ignore his comment about the alcohol.

Our seatmate, who happened to be a professional soccer player from the Los Angeles–based Chivas USA Major League Soccer team added, "That's right. Moms always know best." We were flanked by his teammates on all sides, and these young, energetic athletes kept Christian entertained with sports talk until he gently drifted off to sleep.

This was my first time being away from Charlotte, and I was already missing her like crazy, even though I knew she was in good hands with my mom while Michael was in Texas for the week. The production company offered to cover the expense of one adult companion ticket along with Christian's plane ticket and the cost of an additional plane ticket for Charlotte on such short notice was way more than we could afford. My mom would have her hands full taking care of Charlotte, our two wheaten terriers, and my real estate transactions while we were away, but I had no doubt that she could handle it. After all, she had taught me everything I knew about parenting and selling real estate.

By the time we touched down at Logan International Airport in Boston, it was already well past Christian's bedtime, yet he had plenty of energy to play baseball in the baggage claim area with our new soccer-player friends. The professional athletes took turns pitching his favorite foam ball to him and chased him around the bases while I conversed with their coach, Robin Fraser. Robin and I had met briefly many years before when he was a player on the U.S. Men's National Soccer Team, and I was the director of promotional events for the U.S. World Cup '94 Organizing Committee. As we were preparing to go our separate ways, Robin handed me his business card.

"Definitely let me know if your son ever switches to soccer because we look for kids with passion like that."

His comment made me wonder if Christian's baseball obsession was a passing phase or here to stay.

It was nearly 11 P.M. by the time we picked up our rental car and embarked on the three-hour drive to our final destination in Cape Cod where the movie was being filmed. While en route to our hotel in Hyannis Port, I received a call from a production coordinator instructing us to be on the set at 9 A.M. the following day. Knowing that the odds of Christian being able to function on less than eight hours of sleep were slim, I naively asked if we could make his call time a little later. I quickly learned that we were just one small cog in the movie-making machine, and the schedule that had been set long before our arrival was not about to be changed.

I spent the remainder of the drive envisioning every possible thing that could go wrong. *Would he be able to catch the ball on cue? Would he be scared by the pressure? Would he completely freak out if they tried to get him out of his baseball uniform and into real clothes?* Life with a toddler is always full of surprises, but a lack of sleep is generally a recipe for disaster, and he was about to get considerably less sleep than the 10 hours he needed. The fact that Christian had just sworn off diapers a few weeks prior to our trip added even more uncertainty to the mix.

The only information we had been given about the movie was that Adam Sandler would be playing the role of a deadbeat dad who shows up at his son's wedding, and Christian was to play a member of the wedding party in a baseball game. Adam Sandler had launched his movie career in the mid-1990s with the very successful mass-appeal comedies *Billy Madison* and *Happy Gilmore*. By 2011 Adam had starred in more than 20 movies, many of which he also wrote and produced under the umbrella of his own production company, Happy Madison. His films were not generally critics' favorites; however, his success at the box office was never in doubt because his films had collectively earned $2.5 billion worldwide at the time.

Coincidentally I was once seated in front of Adam at a Los Angeles Kings' game in my mid-20s, and had found him to be just as friendly and approachable as he appeared on the big screen. Our paths were about to cross again, and this time we both happened to be in our early 40s and parents of two children around the same ages. It made perfect sense to me that Adam would choose a family-friendly place like Cape Cod to spend his summer doing what he loved—creating movies that make people laugh.

I was bleary-eyed by the time we checked in to our hotel. The graveyard-shift receptionist handed me an envelope with my name on it, and inside was a production schedule for the following day and handwritten instructions to be at the front of the hotel at 8:30 A.M. the following morning to be transported to the movie set. The filming location was listed as "Mini Fenway Park." Out of curiosity, I asked the night-shift receptionist if he knew where that was. In a thick Boston accent he answered, "Fenway Park is the stadium in Boston where the Red Sox play, but I've never heard of no Mini Fenway Park around here." I didn't bother inquiring further because I figured we would find out for ourselves in a few short hours.

Prominently placed on the reception counter was a stack of schedules for the summer Cape Cod Baseball League games. I'm not sure if it was my extended glance at the display or Christian's baseball uniform that prompted the receptionist to say, "You oughta check out a game or two while you're here. The most talented high school baseball players from all over the country come to the Cape every summer to play ball. I'd bet money that you'll see some of these kids in the Major Leagues real soon." Apparently we had just arrived in baseball Heaven, not so much for me, but for Christian.

The next morning, I managed to get my groggy son out of bed, dressed, and fed in time for the 8:30 A.M. pickup. The large, white van was waiting when we walked out and the first person to greet us was a bubbly woman named Lynn, Christian's "studio teacher." Lynn explained that her job was to make sure that Christian did not "work" more than two hours per day with a maximum of four hours on the set, as dictated by the Screen Actors Guild child labor laws. Lynn's peaceful demeanor was exactly what I needed to quell my fears about how the day would go and whether or not Christian would crumble under the pressure of having to perform on cue. I told her about my fear of Christian having a giant meltdown if they tried to get him to change out of his baseball pants, oversize Red Sox jersey, and cleats.

"I'm sure it will work out just fine," she laughed. I smiled and nodded in agreement, but I wasn't so sure.

Christian's eyes lit up when he saw the movie set. It was a pristine baseball field with freshly laid turf and his favorite red dirt, just like the dirt at Dodger Stadium. The production company had obviously spared no expense in building this Little League–size version of a Major League Baseball stadium. Encompassing the outfield was a 30-foot-high green wall adorned with sponsor logos. A replica of a CITGO gas sign had been constructed to peer over the center-field wall, similar to the real Fenway Park, home of the Boston Red Sox. No wonder our hotel receptionist had never heard of Mini Fenway Park. It was an oasis built specifically for a five-minute scene in a Hollywood movie, and it would be torn down as soon as the shoot was over.

We were greeted at the field by an assistant director telling us that this would be a rehearsal day for Christian. Then we were joined by five former collegiate and professional athletes in their 20s and 30s, who were responsible for orchestrating what I had guessed to be a one-million-dollar baseball scene. Christian enthusiastically pulled his baseball glove, bat, and helmet out of his backpack, eager to play ball on this little field of dreams.

A guy who was wearing a baseball glove introduced himself as Mike, one of the owners of Sports Studio. Mike positioned Christian between first base and second base, and told him that his job was to scoop up the ground balls as they rolled to him, and then throw them to the girl, Carri, who was standing on first base. I was already impressed with Carri's athletic abilities before learning that she was the softball coach at Harvard University. A cameraman filmed the action on the field while I shot videos with my camera to capture the moment. As Christian scooped up ground ball after ground ball, and threw them back with accuracy, Mike yelled with enthusiasm, "There are ten-year-olds that can't do this!"

A steady flow of people, who appeared to be part of the film production crew, kept filtering in until there was a sizable crowd gathered at the baseball field. All eyes were focused on Christian, and it was obvious that he loved the attention of being center stage. At least one of my fears was put to rest. Mike then instructed a crew member to bring a ladder over to first base so they could film Christian catching balls. They repeated this exercise more than 20 times in a row and, against all odds, Christian caught every fly ball. I breathed a sigh of relief when he passed the test. This was the first time I was told that the role Christian was cast for was originally written with a five- to six-year-old boy in mind. Mike told me they had been holding casting calls in Boston for a few weeks for young baseball players before they came across the YouTube video of Christian playing baseball. They say luck is when preparation meets opportunity, but in this particular case, it was all about timing.

When it was time for Christian to take his required breaks, the studio teacher, Lynn, made her best effort to get him to put down his baseball gear and rest. She quickly learned there was no hope of getting him to eat, rest, or stop playing baseball when he was in Baseball Konrad mode. I let Lynn know that playing baseball could never be considered "work" for Christian and as long as it wasn't a violation of the Taft-Hartley Act, I was fine with allowing him to continue hitting balls on the sidelines during his breaks. Christian successfully recruited a friendly, unassuming guy named Kevin to pitch balls to him. We discovered that in addition to being a Boston Red Sox fan, Kevin was also a producer on the film and had been a close friend of Adam Sandler's since their high school days together.

In between pitches, I asked Kevin the big question that had been weighing on my mind ever since I got the call from casting.

"Is there any chance that he will be able to wear his baseball uniform for the actual movie shoot?"

His answer was not what I was hoping to hear.

"Fraid not. Wardrobe will get him set up with clothes and shoes."

I told Kevin about Christian's fixation on his baseball uniform and joked, "The trip to the wardrobe department may be the end of his short-lived movie career."

Kevin shook his head and smiled, "Nah, you see the way he loved the crowds? The boy's a natural."

Regardless of what was to happen with Christian's potential movie debut, we were thoroughly enjoying our all-expenses-paid vacation in Cape Cod. The seaside town of Hyannis Port is an affluent community where Northeasterners flock for the summer, and is best known as the location of the Kennedy family's compound. It was a perfect place to be stranded over the next few days while we waited for news from the production company as to when Christian would need to report back for duty on the set. With the exception of a couple of rainy days, our days and nights in Cape Cod were filled with baseball. Baseball at the beach, baseball in the hotel room, and baseball on a myriad of baseball fields, which were plentiful in the Cape.

We found ourselves at more than a few Cape Cod Baseball League games, where we rooted for teams like the Hyannis Harbor Hawks and the Chatham Anglers. I was pitching balls to Christian in a batting cage at the Hyannis Port stadium when we overheard somebody say the Yankees were coming to Boston in two days to play the Red Sox at Fenway Park. Because we were on standby for the movie shoot, it was a little risky to fork out $150 for the cheapest available ticket, but I took the leap of faith and bought it anyway—figuring Christian was still young enough to sit on my lap. Within hours of making the purchase, we received word from the production company that tomorrow was the day we had been waiting for. Christian would finally be filming his baseball-playing cameo role in the movie. Assuming his role in the baseball scene would take only one day to shoot, we would miraculously be able to make it to the Red Sox game before our return trip to Los Angeles.

On the day of filming, the atmosphere on set was a stark contrast to the laid-back environment of the rehearsal. The white van dropped us off at what looked like a makeshift village packed with trailers and people buzzing around in all directions. Like in a colony of ants, each person appeared to be on a distinct mission. We were met by the assistant director, who immediately sent us to the dreaded wardrobe department. The wardrobe assistant's efforts to get Christian out of his baseball clothes and into the polo shirt, khaki shorts, and dress shoes that he was to wear for the scene were met with a screaming, kicking fit, just as I had feared. He cried so hard that he threw up on the lady, but luckily, not on the new clothes he was wearing.

Our next stop was the makeup department, where a scar on Christian's forehead from a collision with our coffee table a few months earlier was magically disguised. The very funny and talented Tony Orlando (as in the song "Tie a Yellow Ribbon Round the Ole Oak Tree" from the 1970s) was seated next to Christian getting his makeup applied for his role as a self-indulgent billionaire with a mini Fenway Park in his backyard. Within minutes, Tony had Christian laughing and totally oblivious to how much he hated his new clothes. The only remnants of the wardrobe fiasco were Christian's puffy, red eyes.

Kevin, the producer we had met at the rehearsal a few days earlier, then showed up to walk us over to a tent behind home plate to meet Adam Sandler. Adam put Christian at ease right away with a high five, and then proceeded to ask him questions about baseball while I shot photos and videos of the sweet interaction.

"So, Konrad, can I count on you to hook me up with tickets?" Adam joked. "What team are you going to play for? You're going to play for the Dodgers."

"No!" Kevin objected, "he's going to play for the Red Sox!"

Christian surprised us all when he shook his head from side to side and said, "I play for the Yankees."

Adam Sandler made his team of choice known when he gave Christian a big hug and proudly said, "That's my boy!" Christian grinned from ear to ear, and I was elated that I had captured the precious exchange on video so he could remember the experience in the years to come.

My first inkling that this might be an R-rated movie was when Adam told us that his two- and four-year-old daughters were in the movie too, but they wouldn't be allowed to watch it until they were out of high school. I waved good-bye to Christian as they took him out to center field near a large, white screen, which appeared to be used for lighting, and braced myself for what might be about to transpire on the baseball field. The roller-coaster ride was about to begin, and there was no turning back at this point.

The director gave the cue for "quiet on the set." When it was perfectly silent, the cameras began rolling. I watched from afar as Christian picked his nose and grabbed his crotch on cue. This was not exactly what I had expected when we boarded the plane to Boston, but it was pretty darn funny. It took a little less than the allotted two hours to shoot Christian's cameo role, and as soon as filming concluded, he begged to change out of his dreaded wardrobe and back into his baseball uniform and cleats. All possible disasters had been averted, and we still had one day to spare before flying home.

The following day we ventured into the city of Boston to watch the Red Sox play their longtime rivals, the New York Yankees, at the *real* Fenway Park. I didn't know at the time that the nearly 100-year-old ballpark was the oldest Major League Baseball stadium still in use. After the shock of paying the unimaginable price of $60 to park our rental car, we walked to Yawkey Way, the main street in front of the stadium, where the pregame festivities were in full force. On game days Yawkey Way closes to traffic in order to make way for the thousands of baseball fans flowing into Fenway Park. The roadway is transformed into an animated pedestrian streetscape teeming with street vendors and revelry.

The baseball-themed carnival atmosphere seemed custom-made for a baseball-obsessed toddler, with the exception of the massive amounts of beer being consumed. Christian was completely in awe of the 10-foot-tall baseball player on stilts, who leaned down to give him a high five. This larger-than-life caricature cheered as Christian delivered strike after strike into an oversize glove at a speed-pitch booth. Christian became a game-day spectacle himself as enthusiastic Red Sox fans took turns pitching balls to him and showering him with applause as he launched balls into the sky with his tiny wooden bat and ran around imaginary bases near the entrance to the stadium.

Entering the hallowed halls of Fenway Park felt like walking back in time. I followed my young son's lead as he wandered over to a vendor who was selling black-and-white photographs of Red Sox players from days gone by. Much to my surprise, Christian begged me to purchase a large photograph of old-time Red Sox players Ted Williams and Bobby Doerr. It struck me as odd that a photo from

1939 was the only thing he had asked me to buy during our entire trip. We had come across many other souvenirs that seemed much more appropriate and fun for a young boy. His obvious love for the photo inspired me to purchase it and have it shipped to our home.

When I took Christian's hand to lead him through the concourse to our seat, something very strange happened. I was stopped in my tracks when, all of a sudden, he wouldn't budge. He was mesmerized by a larger-than-life portrait of a baseball player from days gone by that was hanging on the wall beside us. Next came an outburst that made time stand still. Christian was visibly upset as he waved his little wooden bat at the photograph and repeatedly yelled, "I do not like him. He was mean to me!" This was not a normal two-year-old tantrum, but a passionate display of emotion with real feeling behind it. It was clear to anybody in the vicinity that Christian believed that this man on the wall had done him harm.

Even strangers had no problem interpreting what he was trying to communicate. One man commented as he was passing by, "This kid is on to something because Babe Ruth was a real jerk." I knew nothing about Babe Ruth at the time, but I did recognize him as a famous baseball player from long ago.

Trying to be empathetic to Christian's obvious upset, I calmly asked, "Babe Ruth was mean to you?"

When he said "Yes!" I felt like a deer in headlights and had no idea how to respond. *How do you have rational conversation with a two-year-old who is convinced that a man who died decades before he was born was mean to him?* I somehow managed to calm him down and get him to our seat, but Christian was so agitated that we only made it through the first two innings of the game. As we made our way out of the stadium, I went out of my way to avoid walking by the wall with the towering photo of Babe Ruth on it. When I called Michael to tell him what had happened, the only word I could find to describe the experience was *eerie.*

CHAPTER THREE

TALL LIKE DADDY

"I did not begin when I was born nor when I was conceived. I have been growing, developing, through incalculable myriads of millenniums . . . All my previous selves have their voices, echoes, promptings, in me . . . Oh, incalculable times again shall I be born."

JACK LONDON, *THE STAR ROVER*

When we landed in Los Angeles, all I could think about was getting to my mom's house as quickly as possible to pick up Charlotte. Bubbling with excitement to be reunited with my family, I gabbed on the phone with my mom for the entire 40-minute drive there. We swapped updates on the movie shoot, our real estate transactions, and life in general. By the time we pulled into her driveway, it was a little after 10 P.M., and she was standing outside in anticipation of our arrival with a very sleepy Charlotte nestled under her arm. I was hoping Christian might remain asleep in his car seat for the additional 10-minute ride to our house, but my hopes were dashed when he snapped out of his peaceful slumber and jubilantly shouted, "Grandma!"

Charlotte and Christian were giddy at being reunited, and stayed up well past midnight planning his third birthday party. I had sent out the invitations prior to our trip to Boston, and the party was now just three days away. Charlotte, the budding artist, sketched a cake design while Christian happily offered direction.

"Make it Dodger blue," he instructed. "Draw a baseball field. Don't forget the catcher. Where will the candles go?"

The three of us crammed into Christian's queen-size bed that night, as was our habit, since neither of them liked to sleep alone. It was very crowded, but better than being woken up in the middle of the night by little ones trying to sneak into my bed. Just before dozing off, Christian got a very serious look on his face.

"Mommy . . . I used to be a tall baseball player."

"Do you mean a 'tall baseball player' like Matt Kemp?" I asked, tucking the blankets around him.

"Yep."

I knew the odds of my son actually becoming a professional baseball player were one in a million, but I seized the opportunity to correct his grammar by saying, "Yes, sweetheart, one day you *will be* a tall baseball player."

He fell asleep and so did I—not giving the exchange another thought.

Michael was scheduled to return the following evening for his normal two-day weekend at home before the Monday morning turnaround to Texas. As much as he disliked the weekly traveling, he didn't have much of a choice because the real estate business that we both relied on for our primary source of income had slowed down considerably. Southern California home prices had plummeted to a five-year low, and so had our annual income. Six years earlier we had been riding the wave of steadily increasing home prices, which had allowed us to buy homes, fix them up, and sell them for a profit—in addition to our regular business of representing clients who were buying or selling their own homes. Thankfully I had been able to put some money in the bank at that time to make it through lean times like this.

Before getting married, Michael and I had come up with a plan to split our bills 50/50, and even with our dwindling income, we stuck with our pact. Although somewhat unconventional, it's a system that has always worked for us. Keeping separate bank accounts and contributing equally to our monthly bills allowed us to make independent financial decisions and also ensured that neither of us would ever feel like we were carrying more than our share of the financial burden.

On Friday evening I was pitching balls to Christian from the kitchen while preparing dinner in anticipation of Michael's arrival when Christian blurted out the same thing he had said the night before.

"Mommy, I used to be a tall baseball player."

"Yes, you will be a tall baseball player someday," I said, as I'd said the night before.

Christian was clearly dissatisfied with my reply. With a look of exasperation, he stomped his foot and hollered.

"No! I *was* a tall baseball player—tall like Daddy!"

Was a baseball player? Tall like Daddy? What was my son trying to say to me? Did he mean . . . he couldn't mean . . . *was he trying to tell me that he was a grown-up in a previous lifetime?*

He stomped his foot again, waiting for me to say something, wanting me to understand him. I took a deep breath as I struggled to come up with a response. Trust me when

I say these are not words you want to hear coming out of your toddler's mouth.

I bent down to his level and looked him in the eye, trying to hide the shock on my face and the worry in my voice.

"You were a grown-up? Like Daddy?"

His answer was a resounding "Yes!" The look of relief on his face was undeniable. He had finally made his point.

Having this conversation with my son was as shocking as seeing a ghost walk through our front door, and seemingly as plausible. Christian's obsession with baseball was strange enough as far as I was concerned, given that there was no affinity for the sport in our family, but his new revelation about having been "tall like Daddy" felt like a descent into the rabbit hole. I found myself straddling the great divide between logic and intuition. The concept of reincarnation was diametrically opposed to my rational thoughts and my religious beliefs, yet my heart was telling me not to ignore what Christian was so desperately trying to tell me.

When Michael walked through the door, I was in urgent need of a reality check. Barely saying hello, I immediately flooded him with all the thoughts that were going through my mind, hoping that he would be able to make sense of it all. Michael listened intently as I rehashed Christian's odd statements and behaviors, which were beginning to feel like pieces of a puzzle. We both found ourselves with more questions than answers. *How could a toddler have an emotional reaction to a portrait of a man who had died half a century before his birth?* Christian was not a kid who was prone to temper tantrums—unless, of course, I was dragging him away from a baseball field or attempting to influence his wardrobe choices. His visceral reaction to Babe

Ruth's photograph was totally illogical and completely out of character. We also couldn't wrap our heads around why a young child would be so attracted to a black-and-white photograph of two old-time Red Sox players. I think I must have exhausted Michael because with a weary smile he said, "Let's let it go for now." I simply couldn't. As soon as my family was soundly asleep, I crept downstairs to my office to scour the Internet for information on Babe Ruth and the two Red Sox players—Ted Williams and Bobby Doerr—in the photo that Christian liked so much. My walk back in time revealed that Ted Williams was one of the greatest left-handed hitters in baseball history. He was born in 1918 and passed away in 2002, six years before Christian was born. I learned that Williams had made his debut in the Major Leagues for the Red Sox in 1939, which was four years after Babe Ruth's retirement. I skimmed through the baseball stats, having no clue what all the numbers and percentages meant. And then, regretfully, I came across a story that made my stomach turn.

Apparently Ted Williams's children had ignored their father's dying wish to have his body cremated, and instead chose to have his remains cryogenically frozen, in hopes that future advances in medical technology might make it possible to revive their father and reunite their family. The children had paid more than $100,000 to have their father's head severed from his body and stored in a steel drum filled with liquid nitrogen. The idea of being able to bring a frozen head back to life seemed wildly preposterous, but then again, searching the Internet for a former baseball player, who my nearly three-year-old son may have known in a previous lifetime, felt equally absurd. This was a sure sign that it was time to put my curiosity to rest.

Our weekend culminated with Christian's third birthday party on Sunday afternoon, a low-key gathering of family and close friends at our home, with an inflatable bounce house that attracted kids from all over our neighborhood. The highlight for Christian came when three of his nine-year-old Little League heroes showed up to wish him a happy birthday. He also loved Charlotte's special baseball-theme birthday cake and the catcher's gear he received from my mom. Following the festivities, Michael and I packed our bags for our upcoming travels. He was off to Texas; Charlotte, Christian, and I would be spending the week in Yosemite at an outdoor camp that had been organized by our church.

As a child in Germany, Michael had periodically attended a Lutheran church with his family, but he had grown out of the habit of going to church during his adult life. When I had suggested we join a local Presbyterian church when I was pregnant with Charlotte, he hadn't been thrilled about the idea of attending the required classes to become church members, but had gone along with my plan anyway. Getting him to go to church was a different story. Michael preferred to spend his Sunday mornings playing tennis. He didn't necessarily dislike going to church, but he just didn't see it as a priority; I did. I had eventually given up trying to persuade Michael to join me, Charlotte, and Christian at church on Sunday mornings—except for special occasions, such as a religious holiday or if our kids were singing in the youth choir. It is quite possible that my desire to provide our children with a strong religious education came from my own topsy-turvy path to discovering religion as a child.

Being the only child of a single, working mother who didn't go to church or talk about religion made me wonder what I was missing out on. My first recollection of being in a church was at the age of five when I attended a Catholic service with a family from my neighborhood. I recall imitating my friend Patty as she dipped her fingers into the holy water and then touched her head, heart, and each shoulder while saying, "In the name of the Father, and of the Son, and of the Holy Spirit." Even though I didn't understand what I was doing, it felt special and sacred.

My next significant memory of my friend Patty was when I was six years old and my mother broke the news to me that Patty and her entire family had died in a tragic car accident. Both parents and all five children died instantly when their camper was hit by an oncoming truck on a winding mountain road. When I asked my mother the big question, "What happens when you die?" I could tell by her response that it wasn't a topic she was comfortable talking about.

This experience sparked my curiosity about God and the mystery of life—and death—and what happens after you die. During my elementary school years, I tagged along to churches, synagogues, and temples with just about anyone who was willing to take me—neighbors, friends, babysitters. Being exposed to different belief systems helped me to understand at an early age that all religions share the underlying teachings of love, compassion, forgiveness, faith in a higher power, and a common belief in the existence of a soul that outlives the body. These concepts are what I was thirsty for, and the packaging was less important.

By the time I was in the fourth grade, I attended church every Sunday with my best friend and her family. At the age of 11, of my own volition, I read the entire Bible from cover to cover one summer. This is when I discovered a deep connection with God, a Divine presence who gives me answers when I pray and makes me feel that I am never alone.

This relationship with God is what I'd hoped my own children would someday find. Attending church regularly seemed like the best way to provide Charlotte and Christian with a foundation for nurturing their own relationship with God. I wanted them to be equipped with answers to life's big questions. The enigmatic questions that have puzzled human beings since the beginning of time such as, *What is God? Is there life before and after death? Do our souls survive the death of our bodies? Will we be reunited with our loved ones after this lifetime?*

The accommodations at our church camp were no frills, with no Internet access or television, but we weren't exactly roughing it because I had opted for a room at the lodge, rather than a tent in the woods with our fellow campers. This was about as primitive as I was willing to bear as the sole caretaker of two young kids in the wilderness. The breathtaking sights, sounds, and smells of nature were at our disposal, while we were also able to enjoy the luxury of a private bathroom and clean sheets. Each day began with a loud clanging bell signaling breakfast was about to be served at the main mess hall, immediately followed by an outdoor worship service overlooking the lake. Charlotte joined our church band on stage to play a bongo drum while we communed with God and our fellow parishioners in the wooded sanctuary. This idyllic, slow-paced environment, where the chirping birds replaced the buzz of cell phones, provided a welcome respite from the stimulation of our daily lives.

However, the one thing that followed us wherever we went was Christian's baseball obsession. Thankfully there were plenty of kids at the camp who offered to play baseball with him—morning, noon, and night.

Every night before bed, Christian would entertain Charlotte and me with stories about his proclaimed life as a "tall baseball player." I no longer corrected him by setting his tales in future tense, and I pretended to be a believer. It was as if the floodgates had opened and, whether real or imagined, Christian's candid tales became more and more entertaining and rich with detail. He continued to express his disdain for Babe Ruth and told us what it felt like to play baseball in front of a big crowd. There was no hint of make-believe in his reflections about the past.

"One time I hurt my knee when I was a tall baseball player," Christian explained.

"Did the doctor have to cut it open to fix it?" I inquired.

"No, I just had to take a break."

On our final night at the camp, after singing songs by the campfire and gobbling up s'mores as quickly as we could make them, Christian said something else new, just before falling asleep.

"Mommy . . . when I was a kid before, there was fire in my house."

"Your house was on fire?" I asked.

He adamantly shook his head from side to side.

"No! There was real fire—in the lights!"

After a few more questions, it became clear that he was saying the lamps in his childhood home used fire for illumination. He was quite convincing when he insisted that they were not candles. From this time forward, I stopped judging and started listening—*really listening*—to what he had to say.

CHAPTER FOUR

OLD SOULS

"It's so silly," [Teddy] said. "All you do is get the heck
out of your body when you die. My gosh, everybody's
done it thousands and thousands of times. Just
because they don't remember it doesn't mean
they haven't done it. It's silly."

J.D. SALINGER, "TEDDY"

As our summer break came to a close, Michael's consulting job with Lockheed Martin ended just as abruptly.
Although losing the steady income was a financial setback,
it was a blessing to have our entire family living under one
roof again. Charlotte was looking forward to starting kindergarten, and I was excited at the prospect of Christian
attending preschool three days per week so I would have
a few mornings to devote to working, rather than playing
baseball.

On the eve of the first day of school, our son, who
had never before expressed interest in television, spotted
a baseball documentary on PBS as I was flipping through
channels to find a children's show for Charlotte. It was the
first time that he had ever glanced in the direction of the
television for more than a few seconds, so I immediately

pressed the Record button on our DVR. As inconsequential as it may sound, this new development was a life-changing event. Despite my previous attempts to entice Christian to watch television so that I could get a break from his never-ending demands to play baseball, this was the first time a television show had ever captured his attention. It was an episode of the Ken Burns documentary miniseries *Baseball*, "The Ninth Inning," a chronicle of Major League Baseball from 1970 to 1990, and from that moment onward, it became Christian's beloved companion and my much needed babysitter for as long as it could hold his interest, sometimes up to an hour per day.

Christian's preschool teacher, Mrs. B, noticed after the first few days of school that Christian was very different from the other students she had taught over the years. Mrs. B was not overly concerned about his unique wardrobe fixation—he insisted on wearing a full baseball uniform to school every day—but she was worried about his detachment from his peers and his unwillingness to engage in typical developmental play. Rather than trying to fit a square peg into a round hole, she embraced Christian's idiosyncrasies and managed to find creative ways to lure him into participating in group activities by tailoring them to his fascination with baseball. If an art project required painting pictures of animals, Mrs. B would encourage Christian to paint a baseball. She even made a special round carpet that looked like a baseball for him to sit on so that he would join his classmates for story time. Michael and I contemplated telling her about Christian's claims of being a "tall baseball player" and asking her professional opinion on whether or not we should be worried, but decided against it out of fear that other families at the

Christian-faith-based preschool would get wind of it and think that we were crazy.

Then something happened that made us question our own sanity. One evening after school, I went to meet Michael at a party at the Mercedes-Benz dealership in Calabasas while Charlotte was at an art class nearby. The only thing Michael loves more than the game of tennis is luxury automobiles. Even though looking at fancy cars wasn't my idea of entertainment, I agreed to join him. Christian was sound asleep in the car by the time he and I arrived at the underground parking lot of the three-story Mercedes-Benz dealership, so I carried him, half-asleep in my arms, to the elevator. When he saw the elevator doors open, he leapt out of my arms and raced to press the button, a habit he had developed from competing with his big sister.

Glancing at the walls and ceiling of the elevator, Christian remarked, "This elevator kind of looks like a hotel."

"Mmm-hmmmm." I nodded.

"When I was a tall baseball player—tall like Daddy—I used to stay in hotels almost every night."

I was startled, hearing this new bit of odd information, but I went along with his story to get more.

"Did you fly on airplanes?"

Christian replied in a matter-of-fact tone, "No, mostly trains."

Our conversation in that elevator is forever etched in my memory, as crystal clear and distinct as the moment he was born.

Hearing these words come out of my three-year-old son's mouth froze time for me, and my mind raced with confusion. *How could he know that baseball players travel to games and stay in hotels? Where in the world did his comment about trains come from? I don't recall any of this information being in the documentary he loved to watch.* Christian had been to only three Major League Baseball games in his life, did not watch baseball games on television, and had never been on a train or expressed interest in playing with toy trains. This is the moment when I started to think that Christian's colorful musings about his life as a baseball player in a former life might be grounded in reality.

When the elevator door opened, I grabbed Christian's hand and raced to find Michael. This time I wasn't sure he'd be able to provide a sanity check. We found him sitting in the driver's seat of a showroom Mercedes-Benz, sipping champagne and chatting with the sales manager. Christian hopped into the backseat of the car, and I told Michael about our strange conversation in the elevator. Michael was just as perplexed by Christian's comments about hotels and trains as I was, and said out loud what I was thinking.

"Wouldn't it be weird if Babe Ruth traveled on trains?"

Our conversation was interrupted by a scantily clad model offering champagne—a perfect excuse to drop the subject and try to forget about what had just happened in the elevator.

Later that evening I went to my computer and Googled: *did babe ruth travel on trains?* I was bombarded by images of Babe Ruth and his Yankees teammates traveling on trains. I read that all professional baseball teams traveled by train during Babe Ruth's era—from 1914 through 1935—and that it wasn't until the mid-1940s that players were given the option of flying to their away games. I shared this new discovery with Michael, and together we searched for a rational explanation as to where Christian could have gotten this information. Ruling out the possibility of a lucky guess, we assumed he must have learned it from the Ken

Burns baseball documentary he had been watching for the past couple of months.

The following day Michael and I watched the entire episode of the Ken Burns miniseries from beginning to end, hoping to solve the mystery. But the film didn't contain any references to baseball history prior to 1970. We decided to investigate other ways Christian may have come across the information. The only times he had ever been out of our care since being born were on the rare occasions when my mom would babysit, or while he was at preschool. After my mom and Mrs. B assured us that he hadn't learned any baseball trivia under their watch, Michael and I were both convinced that there was no possible way that Christian could be getting this information from outside sources. Mrs. B advised us not to dismiss our son's comments as fantasy.

"Kids at this age are much closer to God," she said. "Their hearts are pure love."

Before having children of my own, I often looked into the eyes of a young child and felt an old soul staring back at me. I frequently used the term "old soul" to describe children who appeared to have an unexplainable wisdom beyond their years. But now . . . having my own son tell me historically accurate things about a time long before he was born felt downright creepy. The leap from "old soul" to "reincarnation" was one that I was reluctant to take because it directly conflicted with my Christian beliefs. I had always been taught that the final destination of the soul after death is Heaven. Despite my internal battle of beliefs, I was determined to figure out what was going on with our son.

My quest for answers led me to a woman named Carol Bowman, who wrote the book *Children's Past Lives: How*

Past Life Memories Affect Your Child. I came across her name when reading an old ABC News article from 2005 about her work with a young boy named James Leininger. This boy gave his parents extremely specific information about his previous life as a fighter pilot in World War II—so specific that his parents were able to identify the man as James Huston, Jr. Even James Huston's 78-year-old sister believed James Leininger was the reincarnated soul of her deceased brother because the young boy revealed personal details about her family that nobody could have known. The story resonated with me because the little boy's obsession with planes was similar to Christian's obsession with baseball.

James Leininger's parents reported that by the age of two, their son's every waking moment revolved around planes and war. They said it was mostly before bed when James was drowsy that he would reveal extraordinary details about his former life. This observation caught my attention because Christian's statements about being a "tall baseball player" had always surfaced just as he was falling asleep or right after he woke up. According to therapist Carol Bowman, this was one of the common patterns among children who report past-life memories. After reading that Carol had worked with the Leininger family to help James overcome terrifying nightmares about dying in a plane crash, I immediately clicked over to her website to learn more.

I was a little put off when I clicked on a tab on the home page that read, *Past Life Regression Therapy.* As I read the information, it became evident that Carol was advocating the use of hypnotherapy to access supposed past lives, something that was way out of my comfort zone.

My next click was on a tab that read, *Children's Past Lives*. This is where I found an overview of Carol Bowman's 25 years of research on the topic of young children who recall past lives. Carol's bio said her interest in the study of children's past-life memories began when each of her own children expressed knowledge of having lived before. The website offered two options for parents who thought their child might be recalling a past life: the first was to join a public forum, and the second was to contact Carol directly. I ruled out the option of sharing our story with strangers and instead chose to send Carol Bowman a private e-mail, desperately hoping she would be able to shed some light on our situation. On a deeper level, I may have actually been seeking validation from Carol that we weren't crazy for considering the possibility that Christian's stories about the past were true.

Carol's response to my e-mail arrived in less than 24 hours, and I held on to every word as if I was back in college at UCLA, listening to one of my professors speak on a subject I knew nothing about. Carol stated in her e-mail that children who remember past lives frequently refer to a time when they were "big" or "tall," just as Christian had. She said one of the most difficult aspects of children talking about these memories is the state of shock parents go into when they realize their child is indeed remembering a previous life.

"If Christian says anything more," she wrote, "just take a few deep breaths, and then keep the conversation going."

This feeling of shock she had described was something I could totally relate to because I had experienced it on more than one occasion over the past few months, and so had Michael.

Carol went on to say, "Children's past-life memories can manifest as unlearned talents, abilities, and knowledge—as exhibited by your son. Or sometimes children may show an obsession with WWII airplanes, toy soldiers, boats, playing a particular instrument, horses, or anything that connects to their former lives."

She found Christian's story fascinating because his attraction to the sport of baseball was clearly not something that we had initiated, or that we had taught him.

"Christian's natural talent for baseball at such a young age is the most telling," Carol concluded. "It is highly likely that he acquired these skills in a former lifetime as a baseball player."

Her words confirmed what I had been thinking and threw my mind into a tailspin. Carol suggested that we try to figure out who he had been by showing him photos of teams Babe Ruth had played with. She said it was important not to prompt him, and just show him photos and see if he recognized his former self.

"Don't worry about reading too much into it. I know this is new territory for you. Just be a careful observer and write down everything that Christian says about his previous lifetime. If he's in the mood to talk about the past, it's fine to encourage him by using open-ended questions, as I describe in my book. Don't worry about planting suggestions because he can override any suggestions that aren't accurate."

Carol encouraged me to do this sooner than later because there is a very small window of time when children talk about the past and these memories are accessible. She said that by the age of six, the specific memories generally tend to fade, although a child may continue to have the talents, interests, and other personality traits that have carried forward from the past. This was certainly new territory for me, but the signs were too big to ignore.

CHAPTER FIVE

THE GRUDGE

"Forgiveness is not always easy. At times, it feels more painful than the wound we suffered, to forgive the one that inflicted it. And yet, there is no peace without forgiveness."

MARIANNE WILLIAMSON

During the fall of 2011, Christian's candid storytelling about his proclaimed life as a baseball player from another era had become an evening ritual as predictable as our bedtime prayers. With Charlotte and me as his captive audience, Christian vividly described his life as a "grown-up baseball player" during a time he referred to as the "olden days." He told us that the Dodgers used to play in New York, which he never could have known, and further surprised me by saying, "We played our games during the day because there were no lights on the field in the olden days."

Following Carol Bowman's recommendation, I kept track of Christian's remarks by writing them down in a notebook that I kept on a bookshelf beside his bed. When researching the accuracy of the things he had told us, I was amazed to find that every detail he had shared turned out to be true. The Dodgers were, in fact, based in Brooklyn,

New York, prior to moving to Los Angeles in 1957, and the first night game ever played under lights at Yankee Stadium was in 1946, long after Babe Ruth's retirement from baseball. The consistency and historical accuracy of Christian's statements led me to believe that there could be something more to this than pure coincidence.

For the most part, Michael and I went about the business of our daily lives that fall, and I kept quiet about the growing inner conflict I felt between my Christian beliefs and the mounting evidence that our son could truly be accessing a past life. We were not horribly concerned about any of his strange revelations, except when it came to the topic of his lingering grudge toward Babe Ruth. His dislike for the man was so intense that Charlotte soon figured out that the most effective way to upset her little brother was by calling him "Babe Ruth." After slinging these words, Charlotte would run away and lock herself in the nearest bathroom to avoid Christian's hair-pulling retaliation. Even Michael, who didn't normally get too involved in disputes between the kids, thought it was incredibly bizarre that Christian was so deeply affected by the mention of Babe Ruth's name. It was clear to us this was not an act to get attention because Christian's emotional upset and tears were very real.

Michael and I were in agreement that something extremely strange was going on with our son, but we had different opinions on how to handle it. I asked Michael what he thought of Carol Bowman's idea of showing Christian photos of players from Babe Ruth's era to see if he could recognize his former self. Even though I wasn't 100 percent sold on the idea that our son had actually lived a previous life as a "tall baseball player," I have to admit, the thought of trying to figure out which player he was claiming to be had crossed my mind long before Carol Bowman had suggested it.

"I bet he'll stop talking about it all if you just ignore him when he brings it up," Michael pleaded.

I, on the other hand, thought that getting our son to open up more would help him let go of his irrational anger toward Babe Ruth. This was the main thing fueling my curiosity.

Ignoring Michael's advice, I began my expedition into uncharted territory by searching for photos of baseball teams from Babe Ruth's era, as Carol had recommended. I printed the black-and-white photos and tucked them into the notebook beside Christian's bed. As predictable as the setting sun, that evening before bed Christian said out of the blue, "Babe Ruth was not nice, Mommy."

On cue, I carefully pulled out a black-and-white photo of the 1927 Yankees team and handed it to Christian without saying a word. Studying it closely, he pointed to Babe Ruth and said, "There's dumb Babe Ruth."

"Do you think there are any players on this team who don't like Babe Ruth?" I gently asked. Although he had 30 players to choose from, Christian immediately pointed to a stocky guy with big dimples and said with confidence, "Him!"

Pointing to the same player, I asked, "Do you know him?"

He looked into my eyes and said, "That's me."

Charlotte giggled, and I hid my astonishment by taking a moment to rustle through the stack of photos. I felt like running out of the room but remembered Carol Bowman's advice to stay calm. I pulled out a few more team pictures and asked Christian if he could find any other baseball players who didn't like Babe Ruth. He pointed to the same stocky guy with dimples in every photo.

As soon as Charlotte and Christian dozed off, I hurried downstairs to my office and Googled: *1927 yankees dimples*. My Internet search identified the man who Christian had pointed out in the photos as Lou Gehrig. The only thing I knew about Lou Gehrig, aside from the fact that he had played for the New York Yankees with Babe Ruth, was that he had died of an illness later named after him—Lou Gehrig's disease—also known as amyotrophic lateral sclerosis, or ALS. I was already confused enough by my son claiming to be a professional baseball player in a past life, but having him say that he was a player who had died of a horrific, incurable disease was even more incomprehensible.

Ironically Christian had received three vintage, hand-painted baseball plates for his third birthday two months earlier from my good friend Wendy, and one of them was an image of Lou Gehrig giving his retirement speech at Yankee Stadium. I had tucked the Lou Gehrig plate away for safekeeping, rather than displaying it in Christian's bedroom, because I found the fact that Lou Gehrig had died such a horrible death somewhat depressing. Now this man who I'd literally put in the closet two months prior had just become the central focus of my investigation to figure out who my son may have been in a former life—despite the fact that I still wasn't sure if I believed in reincarnation.

Before heading to bed, I clicked on the Google Images search for Lou Gehrig, and came across several photos of Lou Gehrig and Babe Ruth hugging. To my relief these photos did not fit with Christian's theory that the man with the dimples didn't like Babe Ruth. Perhaps he was making up some of his stories after all. I printed a few photos of the two men together so I could show them to Christian before bed the following evening. Maybe seeing the photos would help him let go of his acrimonious feelings toward Babe Ruth.

As expected Christian started the dialogue about Babe Ruth and Lou Gehrig before bed the following evening. I seized the opportunity to introduce the photos of Babe and Lou with their arms around each other. Perhaps this would convince Christian that Babe Ruth wasn't such a bad guy after all. The first photo I showed him was of Lou Gehrig and another man in a Yankees uniform, who I thought was Babe Ruth. Christian studied the photo and said, "That's not dumb Babe Ruth. That's the coach."

After looking at the fine print below the photo, I was stunned that Christian was right; the man standing beside Lou Gehrig in the photo was former Yankees skipper Joe McCarthy, not Babe Ruth. Christian could recognize only a few letters at the time and did not know how to read, so I knew there was no chance of him being able to read the fine print. I was starting to think he might actually be recognizing these people, but I still wasn't sold on the idea that he *was* Lou Gehrig. Besides being totally outside my realm of thinking, it also didn't explain Christian's grudge toward Babe Ruth. Babe Ruth and Lou Gehrig appeared to be quite fond of each other in the photos I had found.

When the kids fell asleep that night, like clockwork, I resumed my Internet investigation. I wanted to get to the bottom of Christian's Babe Ruth grudge, so I feverishly Googled: *who disliked babe ruth?* I came upon a story about Babe Ruth's long-running battle with Ty Cobb, a man who the article said was universally disliked by his opponents and many of his own teammates. I gathered from the same article that Babe Ruth was not necessarily a "real jerk," as the people passing by Christian's emotional outburst at Fenway Park had said, but history had painted him as somewhat of a swashbuckling glutton, prone to a life of excess.

Then I stumbled across something that sent jolts of electricity through my body and made the hair on my head stand on end. It was an article that perfectly explained Christian's animosity toward Babe Ruth, if Christian was indeed Lou Gehrig, as he had asserted. I read that, in addition to being teammates and two of the best left-handed hitters of all time, Lou Gehrig and Babe Ruth were the best of friends until they had a major falling-out. The article reported that Lou and Babe went from being traveling companions, golf partners, and bridge buddies to totally ignoring each other on and off the field, despite playing for the same team day in and day out. I read the first time the two men acknowledged each other in seven years was on July 4, 1939, when Lou Gehrig announced his retirement from baseball at Yankee Stadium.

The article went on to describe how an entire nation was moved to tears by the inspiring words of a man facing his imminent demise from the ravaging effects of ALS. While wiping away his own tears, Lou Gehrig said, "Today I consider myself the luckiest man on the face of the Earth. And I might have been given a bad break, but I've got an awful lot to live for." The baseball hero took his final breath two years later at the age of 37.

The article reported that Lou Gehrig's wife became very angry when Babe Ruth showed up intoxicated to Lou's funeral. A family friend was quoted as saying of Babe Ruth's appearance that day, "He certainly wasn't wanted by the Gehrigs, as there was friction between them for years."

This discovery of the feud between the two men was so shocking that I immediately rushed upstairs to tell Michael. I found him sound asleep on the couch with a remote in his hand and a tennis match blaring on the television. I touched Michael's shoulder to wake him and the startled look on his face matched my emotions at that moment. Without thinking, I blurted out:

"Michael, I think Christian really was Lou Gehrig."

As soon as the words fell out of my mouth, I wanted to take them back. It wasn't until I heard my words out loud that I realized how irrational I sounded.

Michael gave me a confused look and said, "Rewind." I rattled off the details that led me to make this preposterous declaration. I told him how Christian had correctly identified Joe McCarthy as the coach of the Yankees, and about the feud between Lou Gehrig and Babe Ruth.

"And then when I showed him a photo of Lou Gehrig," I took a steadying breath, "Christian pointed to his face and said . . . 'That's ME.'"

Michael looked intrigued by my hypothesis, but then begged, "Let's go to bed and *not* talk about this in the morning, okay?"

So we retired for the night and I tossed and turned, for what seemed like hours, with the image of Christian angrily waving his tiny bat at the towering picture of Babe Ruth flashing through my mind.

CHAPTER SIX

FINDING
LOU GEHRIG

"I never heard of [Lou] Gehrig before I came here
and I always thought Babe Ruth was a cartoon
character. I really did. I mean, I wasn't
born until 1961 and I grew up in Indiana."

Don Mattingly, Yankees legend and MLB manager

I didn't bring up the topic with Michael the next morning because I knew he had been half-serious the night before when he had said *let's not talk about it.* Michael was as interested in talking about our son's claims of being Lou Gehrig as he was in talking about anything having to do with baseball—not at all. Ironically, just as I was beginning to believe Christian and wanted to talk about it more, Michael wanted to shut down the conversations.

After dropping Christian off at preschool, I crossed paths with two of my closest mom-friends in the school parking lot. After a split-second decision, I proceeded to tell them about the stories Christian had shared with us over the past few months. Sarah and Wendy had been my faithful confidantes in the arena of parenting ever since we all met at a mommy-and-me class when our first-born children were still in diapers. I was hoping they might be able to help me navigate the murky waters of uncertainty. Although they were both privy to every other intimate detail of my life, it took a great deal of courage for me to open up about this particular secret. It was just so personal.

Our interaction turned south as soon as I told Sarah and Wendy about Christian saying he had "stayed in hotels almost every night" and had traveled on trains when he was "tall like Daddy."

"Aw, c'mon, Cathy," Wendy said with disbelief, "He could have picked that up anywhere."

Sarah laughed and added, "I'm sure he's making that stuff up. That's what three-year-olds do."

I ached to believe that they were right, but I couldn't deny what I knew in my heart to be true. There was no possible way that Christian could have known these things. Wendy, a devout Christian, then said something that cut through me like a knife.

"You don't want to be on the wrong side of God, Cathy."

I was already feeling guilty for believing my son when he said he'd lived before, but now this?

When my friends didn't provide the comfort I was seeking, I turned to my mom for support. In addition to telling her all the things Christian had shared with us about being a baseball player in the 1920s, I also shared with her how shattered I was when Sarah and Wendy dismissed my overtures in the school parking lot. My mom found Christian's revelations oddly coincidental. However, her advice was to stop dwelling on it—both Christian's stories, and my need to convince Sarah and Wendy that Christian was not fantasizing.

I heeded my mom's advice to ignore it and wish it away for a few days, until I could no longer ignore the persistent nagging in my heart to search for answers. I wanted to know more about this man Lou Gehrig, whom our son had grown so fond of. I knew from my research that Lou Gehrig's primary claim to fame, aside from his untimely death from ALS, was his uninterrupted run as the starting first baseman for the Yankees for 2,130 consecutive games during the 1920s and '30s, but I wanted to know more about the man behind the legend.

Every description I read of Lou Gehrig referred to him as the "Iron Horse," a nickname he had acquired as the result of his unrivaled work ethic and his plethora of batting records, some of which have never been broken. Lou Gehrig was not only revered for his tremendous feats on the ball field, but also for his outstanding character and squeaky-clean reputation. While Babe Ruth was a poster child for the excessive drinking and womanizing that symbolized the 1920s, Lou Gehrig stayed away from trouble. He prided himself on going to bed early and getting 9–10 hours of sleep, while his teammates were out partying into the wee hours of the night. Lou lived at home with his parents until he was 30 years old. His passion for baseball was conveyed by a sportswriter who wrote in 1927, "They say that Lou Gehrig would rather play ball than eat, which is saying a lot for any ball player." I found this quote especially humorous because the same could be said of Christian.

When I read that Lou Gehrig was born in 1903, it brought to mind the comment that Christian had made at church camp about having "real fire in the lights" when he was "a kid before." I had never been a big history buff, so I had no idea how homes were lit in the early 1900s. When

I looked it up, I discovered that Lou Gehrig was born long before electricity lit up the streets of New York. The conversion from gas lighting to electricity wasn't fully completed in New York City until the 1920s, so it was highly likely that Lou Gehrig's childhood home did indeed have "fire in the lights," as Christian had described.

When all roads seemed to lead to Lou Gehrig, I decided to show Christian a photo of Lou Gehrig's parents one night before bed. I was curious to see if he would be able to identify their real names among a list of fictitious names that I had made up.

"Christian, look at the man in this photo. Is his name Joseph?"

"No," he quickly replied.

As I rattled off five more incorrect names, he said no every single time. Then it was time to give him the real name.

"Is this Heinrich?" I asked.

Christian shook his head. "No."

I thought I had stumped him in this guessing game until I read the fine print below the photo, which said Lou's father, Heinrich, went by the nickname "Henry." I pointed to the man in the photo again and asked, "Is this Henry?"

"Yes," Christian calmly said, as if it was common knowledge.

Then I tried my little experiment again by asking him to correctly identify Lou Gehrig's mother. I pointed to the woman in the same photo.

"Is this Mary?" I asked.

Christian confidently replied, "No."

He then said no three more times in response to fake names I ran by him. And then, "Is this Christina?"

"Yes!" He was right again; Christina was her real name.

Staring closer at the photo, Christian looked at the woman's face and said to me, "Why weren't you there then, Mommy? I like you better."

This was by far the strangest thing he had ever said until he topped it a few seconds later by pointing at Christina Gehrig's photo and saying, "Mommy, you were her."

Goosebumps crawled up my arms to the back of my neck, and made my hair stand on end.

Trying to change the subject, I asked Christian if Henry and Christina had had a car. He replied, "Only strangers had cars." Christian then told me and Charlotte that Henry and Christina both smoked, which made Charlotte giggle. I playfully pulled him close for a hug, but I could feel him resisting. He continued to pensively stare at the photo until he interrupted the silence by saying once again, "Mommy, you were her."

I shuddered slightly. It was apparent that Christian wanted to make sure that he had made his point. When I nodded to feign agreement, Charlotte leaned over to whisper in my ear, "Now this is getting really weird."

I didn't give much thought to Christian insisting that I was Christina Gehrig because I figured it was his way of integrating the two worlds he was living in—his alleged past life as a tall baseball player and his current life. However, I was shocked that he was able to correctly identify the names of Lou Gehrig's parents. I was also more than a little surprised when I read that Lou Gehrig's mother had emigrated from exactly the same area in Northern Germany where Michael's parents were born and raised. In another strange twist of fate, my maternal grandmother, like Lou Gehrig, was also a daughter of German immigrants and grew up in a very poor Chicago neighborhood in the early 1900s. I figured it was highly likely that Lou Gehrig's German immigrant family, who had struggled to make ends meet, would be among the last to acquire electricity or an automobile. This fit perfectly with Christian's statement that "only strangers had cars."

I also couldn't get over the uncanny physical similarities between Christian and Lou Gehrig. In addition to their shared German heritage, Christian and Lou were both left-handed and had those prominent dimples, with the one on the left being noticeably deeper than the one on the right. I didn't see this as something significant until Carol Bowman pointed out the physical resemblance between Lou Gehrig and Christian and told me it is quite common for physical traits to carry over from one lifetime to the next.

On the last day of school before Thanksgiving break, I met up with Sarah and Wendy at our favorite breakfast spot to celebrate Sarah's birthday. Against my better judgment, I brought up Christian's past-life stories again. I excitedly shared with them how Christian had correctly identified Lou Gehrig's parents in the photo. The more passionate I was in my plea to win them over, the more distant they both became. They seemed to be united in solidarity, and Sarah even spoke for them both when she curtly said, "You really need to get over this, Cathy."

Her words stung, and I made a conscious decision in that moment to keep my future conversations with Sarah and Wendy limited to lighter subjects.

CHAPTER SEVEN

POSSESSED OR CRAZY

"See that you don't look down on one of these little ones, because I tell you that in heaven their angels continually view the face of my Father in heaven."

MATTHEW 18:10

For the first time in my life, I didn't know what to believe in. I felt as if I was holding on for dear life to a wildly swinging pendulum. My Christian faith dictated that I disregard the reincarnation explanation, and yet my gut was telling me it was somehow feasible. Something beyond my understanding was certainly at play. I was petrified to talk to our church pastor about what was going on, so I instead opted to confide in my good friend Pastor Wyatt to see if he could help me find my way.

Michael and I had originally met Wyatt before we were married, when he joined our Rotary Club. The three of us got to know each other on a deeper level when Wyatt conducted our premarital counseling. We were all bonded for life after he officiated our wedding ceremony on the beach in Malibu. Shortly after our wedding, Wyatt moved to Montana with his wife and daughter to become the head pastor at a Lutheran church. Our communication with Pastor Wyatt dwindled to an annual Christmas card swap, exchanges on Facebook, and an occasional e-mail here and there. Even though Pastor Wyatt's beliefs were far more conservative than my own, neither of us shied away from a good debate on topics of spirituality, and we often agreed to disagree.

My most recent sparring match with Pastor Wyatt centered on his Facebook post about plans to bless a home that was reportedly inhabited by what he referred to as an "evil spirit." When I suggested that the supernatural visitation he described might just be a lingering soul that hadn't found its way to Heaven yet, Pastor Wyatt made it very clear that he believed there was no such thing as a friendly ghost. Our Facebook exchange on the topic came to an end when I commented that I had never encountered a person who struck me as purely "evil" and certainly did not share his view that there was such a thing as an "evil spirit." I was saddened by his perspective but valued our friendship nonetheless.

I carefully composed a four-page letter outlining all the recent incidents that had led me to believe my son may have been a baseball player in a previous lifetime and sent it to Pastor Wyatt via e-mail to get his take on our situation. Right after I clicked the Send button, all my fears flooded in. I thought back to all of the horrific comments I had read on the Internet thread below the story about James Leininger, the young boy who had described a past life as a fighter pilot in World War II. The consensus among conservative Christians on the thread was that the child was in desperate need of an exorcism. I knew in my heart this wasn't true, yet I couldn't seem to get the image of Linda Blair's head-spinning scene from *The Exorcist* out of my mind.

My heart skipped a beat when Pastor Wyatt's response appeared in my in-box a few hours later. There it was in black and white, my worst nightmare realized. Wyatt didn't come right out and say that he thought Christian was either possessed or crazy, but my mind raced to that conclusion under the weight of his words. I felt sick to my stomach after reading the first line, a biblical passage: (Hebrews 9:27) "And just as it is appointed for man to die once, and after that comes judgment."

In my mind this was Pastor Wyatt's attempt to talk me off the cliff and rescue me from my own demise before it was too late. However, this biblical scripture didn't strike me as empirical evidence against the case of reincarnation. *The Bible says "it is appointed for man to die once," but does this preclude a soul from experiencing more than one lifetime?* In the same e-mail, Pastor Wyatt offered to pray for our family and lovingly warned me of the backlash that might come our way if we were to share our son's story with people of faith. The implication seemed to be that people might think our son was possessed by the spirit of a dead person. In closing Wyatt asked, "Wasn't it Art Linkletter who was known for saying, 'Kids say the darndest things'?" I responded to his e-mail by thanking him for his input and prayers, but underneath my pleasantries, I was feeling more conflicted than ever.

I once heard someone say, "You need to get lost in order to find yourself." At 44 years of age, I never imagined myself being this lost. I didn't think I had the energy or the inclination to embark on the journey of finding myself, but this is when the journey found me. Pastor Wyatt's e-mail inspired me to dig deeper into the religious roots of reincarnation. I was particularly interested in finding out why the concept of living more than one lifetime was incompatible with Christianity. My research revealed that nowhere in the Bible is reincarnation addressed, let alone banned. Much to my surprise, I could not find a single scripture in the Bible that repudiates reincarnation—or "rebirth," as it was called in ancient religious teachings.

I was astonished to discover that the concepts of "pre-existence" and "rebirth" were integral to nearly all religions, including Christianity, until A.D. 325 when the Roman emperor, Constantine the Great, decreed speaking about "rebirth" to be an act of heresy against the church. By A.D. 385, the union of church and state was complete, and speaking about reincarnation was no longer just a sin but also a crime punishable by death. The massacres of men, women, and children who promoted the concepts of reincarnation, "rebirth," or "pre-existence" of the soul continued well into the 15th century. By the 16th century, these concepts had been all but wiped out in Christian teachings, with the exception of a few underground mystical groups. *Could the guilt I felt about believing in reincarnation be rooted in this bloody religious persecution that had taken place centuries ago?* I slowly began to forgive myself for stepping outside of my Christian beliefs in my search for answers. This unleashed a new sense of freedom to explore the unknown.

This is when I delved into the work of Dr. Ian Stevenson, a medical doctor and psychiatrist who had dedicated his 40-year career as the head of the Division of Perceptual Studies at the University of Virginia's School of Medicine to investigating the past-life memories and near-death experiences of children. Dr. Stevenson's studies on reincarnation focused on very young children because he felt their limited life experiences made it possible to isolate memories that could only be explained by a past life. In each case he went to great lengths to identify everything a child had been exposed to in order to rule out the possibility that the information had been learned in the current lifetime. Dr. Stevenson's 2,500 documented cases of children who remembered past lives provided hard, scientific evidence that I could sink my teeth into. I liked the fact that he himself was a skeptic and had gone to great lengths to disprove the cases he had investigated.

Dr. Stevenson's discoveries as a parapsychologist had led some to compare him to Darwin and Galileo, both of whom had been scorned and ridiculed by their contemporaries due to their unconventional ideas. Many of Ian Stevenson's colleagues at the University of Virginia had been opposed to the head of their mental health program pursuing paranormal investigations. Yet this had not stopped him in his quest to answer the age-old question: "What survives bodily death?" Stevenson had traveled all over the world to meet families, hear their stories, and determine if the children's memories were valid.

In the end, he had actually convinced himself and others that these recollections, out of the mouths of babes, were the key to scientifically proving the eternity of the soul. According to Stevenson, only a small percentage of children retain any memories of their previous lifetimes. Research by Ian Stevenson's contemporaries David Barker and Satwant Pasricha found that even in India, where nearly everyone believes in reincarnation and it's not considered something out of the ordinary, only about 1 in every 450 recall past lives.

Each of Dr. Stevenson's case studies had followed the same protocol. They had begun with a young child, usually between the ages of two and four, talking about a past life and revealing information about people and places that nobody in the family had ever heard of before. In the majority of cases the recollections had been accompanied by odd behaviors that supported the child's claims. The children he had studied usually persisted in talking about their memories for months or years, even in cases where the child's family had attempted to suppress the memories.

In each case Dr. Stevenson used rigid scientific methods to interview the child while the memories were still fresh. He also extensively questioned the family members to make sure the child could not have learned the reported facts from experiences in his or her current lifetime. Many of the children in Dr. Stevenson's studies had talked about being "big," had recalled vivid events from another lifetime, and had displayed skills beyond their years that were not taught or learned. Some children had even spoken in languages that they had never been exposed to. Dr. Stevenson's criteria for assessing children's past-life memories sounded remarkably similar to the behaviors and statements that our son had been demonstrating.

I felt a little uneasy when I read Dr. Stevenson's theory that a child may inherit birthmarks or birth defects in their current life as a result of ailments or injuries from their previous life. I read that Dr. Stevenson attributed his personal interest in this phenomenon to his own experience of having bronchial tube defects from early childhood. This struck a chord with me because the person who Christian was claiming to be had died young from a deadly disease. Christian did not have any distinctive birthmarks or birth defects, but he did suffer from asthma attacks, which had required visits to the emergency room an average of three to four times per year since he was six months old. In my experience as a mother, there was nothing more grueling than sleepless nights watching our son struggle to breathe. I couldn't help but wonder if there could be some truth to Dr. Stevenson's seemingly far-fetched theory.

I could no longer deny our son's claims of being a baseball player in a past life simply because the concept of reincarnation did not fit with my Christian beliefs. I became less concerned about being criticized by others and more committed to searching for the truth.

This is when I came across a beautiful teaching in the Babylonian Talmud that seemed to make perfect sense. According to this medieval Jewish text, the angel Lailah lives in the womb and watches over the embryo until it is time to be born. The angel teaches the unborn child everything there is to know about the mysteries of life and his or her own soul. When the time comes for the child to be born, the angel Lailah puts her finger in front of her own mouth as if to say "shhh," and then presses the upper lip of the child so all the memories are forgotten. According to the myth, the light touch on the child's lip leaves a small indentation above the lip called a philtrum, which is something we all have. I started to think that perhaps the angel Lailah just hadn't pressed quite hard enough on some children's lips, and this is why they had come into their current life bearing soul memories.

I breathed a sigh of relief when I came across the Watkins' list of the "100 Most Spiritually Influential Living People" for 2011. The list was filled with highly respected gurus who preach the eternity of the soul and the possibility of living more than one lifetime. Pope Benedict XVI didn't even make the top 30, yet number 2 on the list, the

Dalai Lama, is widely believed to be the reincarnated soul of the Buddha of compassion and 14 other Tibetan monks. He had even won a Nobel Peace Prize for his nonviolent opposition to China's occupation of Tibet, which isn't half bad. That night in bed I asked my half-asleep husband, "Do you think anybody ever accused the Dalai Lama of being possessed?"

As he tugged on the covers and rolled deeper into his cocoon, he mumbled under his breath, "Forget about it."

I wasn't able to forget about it, but I did my best to refrain from bringing up the subject with Michael. The approaching holidays provided a much-needed distraction for us both. For Christmas that December, all Christian asked for from Santa were "big, squishy bases" and a machine to make chalk baselines. His wishes came true.

One of the highlights of 2011 was our unexpected delight in watching Charlotte and Christian ride their bikes without training wheels for the first time—not because they had mastered the skill, but due to the sheer joy on their faces when they realized they were balancing on their own. It reminded us that to keep your balance, you must keep moving forward and keep your head up, especially when you feel wobbly. This lesson came in handy for our entire family at this particular time in our lives.

CHAPTER EIGHT

SPRING FEVER

"That's the true harbinger of spring, not
crocuses or swallows returning to Capistrano,
but the sound of a bat on a ball."

Bill Veeck

The following spring our family was introduced to the subculture of Little League baseball. At the ripe age of three and a half, Christian had been waiting more than half of his life for this moment. He was still a few months shy of the minimum age to play Little League T-ball, but I talked our league president into making an exception for our baseball-obsessed son. The grassy fields with their dusty mounds became our new home away from home. Because Malcolm Gladwell's book *Outliers* was quite popular at the time, Michael and I often joked that our three-year-old son was already well on his way to achieving Gladwell's recommended 10,000 hours of practice to master any skill.

The amount of time Christian spent every day hitting, catching, and throwing baseballs was staggering. His little body was in perpetual motion and refused to slow down, even when he was asleep. In the midst of deep sleep, Christian sometimes sat up in bed and said things like, "Fly ball over here!" without waking up. The start of the Little League baseball season provided a welcome outlet for his love of the game, and I secretly hoped the experience of being on a team would distract him from thinking about the Yankees and Lou Gehrig.

Ironically, while Christian was partaking in his first T-ball practice, a video of his batting practice on Adam Sandler's movie set was featured on the MLB Network show *Intentional Talk*. The ex-jock talk-show hosts playfully reported that a three-year-old was being scouted for Red Sox camp. Their tongue-in-cheek report included a review of Christian's stats and an announcement of his baseball-playing cameo role in the soon-to-be-released Adam Sander comedy *That's My Boy*.

The news story on the MLB Network came as a bit of a surprise, but the bigger shock had come a few days earlier when I'd received a call from my half-sister, Laura, while running in the hills near our home. After I answered the call, the first words out of Laura's mouth were, "Christian is in the news!" I thought she was referring to the article that had run in the *Thousand Oaks Acorn* newspaper about Christian's role in the Adam Sandler movie, until it occurred to me that Laura lives in Nashville and I hadn't told her about the article yet. It was surreal to hear that a photo of Christian and Adam Sandler was on the scrolling news stories of the day on the Yahoo home page. This was my first hint that we were about to board a runaway media train that was beyond our control. It seemed our only option at this point was to ride it out and hope the damage would be minimal. I ran back home at record pace, eager to figure out how in the world this had happened.

As it turned out, a local sports writer and radio talk-show host named Ben Maller had read the article about

Christian in our local paper that morning and had used the information to write a story for Yahoo Sports. The headline of Ben's article on the Yahoo home page read: "YouTube Gets 3-Year-Old A Baseball Movie Role." The story included a link to our YouTube video of Christian filming the movie with Adam Sandler. Over the course of two days, the video received more than 800,000 views. By doing a little digging, I found it was not by sheer coincidence that the YouTube video went viral. Yahoo and YouTube were strategic partners at the time, and what we had just experienced was good, old-fashioned cross promotion. Just as I had learned way more than I'd ever intended to know about baseball, I was also learning way more than I had ever wanted to know about YouTube. The parental duty of screening the hundreds of viewer comments, so I could delete any containing profanity, was added to my list of things to do.

In the spring of 2012, Christian's passion for baseball spread like wildfire in our family. Even Michael, who'd had little patience for the baseball scenes in *Moneyball* one year earlier, found himself addicted to those *bottom of the ninth, two outs, two strikes, and the guy hits a game-winning home run* moments. Christian began watching Dodger games on television, and his infatuation with the larger-than-life Major League Baseball players inspired us to become Dodger season-ticket holders. This meant long drives to Dodger Stadium on a weekly basis for beautiful sunsets, fresh air, catching foul balls at batting practice, Friday night fireworks, and more bobbleheads than we could comfortably fit in our home.

Right before the start of the season, the Los Angeles Dodgers had been purchased by Guggenheim Baseball Management for the highest price ever paid for a sports franchise, $2.15 billion in cash. I was excited when I found out that my former employer, Earvin "Magic" Johnson, was one of the new owners of the Dodgers. I hadn't been in close contact with Magic since leaving my job as vice president of the Magic Johnson Foundation 14 years earlier to pursue a career in real estate with my mom, but this serendipitous turn of events provided a great opportunity to rekindle the friendship. When our paths crossed at Dodger Stadium on a Tuesday night, I introduced Magic to Christian and proposed the idea of having him throw a ceremonial first pitch at a Dodger game. Although Magic didn't appear to take the request too seriously, he was amused by my tenacity.

A few days later, I was navigating the aisles of a grocery store with Charlotte and Christian in tow when I received a call from the Dodgers' main office. The person on the other end of the line said he and his colleague, who was also on the line, were calling because they had heard about my request to have my three-year-old son throw a first pitch at a Dodger game. The man then said, "Ma'am, you know that everybody wants their kid to throw a first pitch, right?" At that moment my sense of recognition clicked, and I realized that I was being punked.

I asked with a knowing laugh, "Is this Lon?" It was indeed my old friend Lon Rosen, Magic Johnson's longtime agent, who I had first met when he interviewed me to work at Magic's foundation. As it turned out, Lon was now the executive vice president of marketing for the Los Angeles Dodgers. The three of us had a good laugh, and I even managed to keep my sense of humor when Lon delivered the disappointing news that there was no chance of Christian throwing a ceremonial first pitch at a Dodger game.

His exact words were: "It's not gonna happen."

Since my hopes of having Christian throw a first pitch at a Dodger game were dashed, his preschool teacher, Mrs. B, arranged for him to throw a first pitch at a high school baseball game. Christian had such a good time throwing the first pitch at the high school game that another friend made arrangements for him to throw a first pitch at a Pepperdine University baseball game. Sitting in the dugout with the college players on the beautiful field overlooking the Malibu coastline was like being in Heaven for our little boy. He was right at home on the mound, and his ceremonial first pitch was a big hit with the crowd. We were amazed when two color photos of Christian's first pitch at the Pepperdine University game showed up on the cover of *The Malibu Times* newspaper the following week with the headline, "Watch Your Back Clayton Kershaw." We had no idea who Clayton Kershaw was at the time, but easily deduced that he must have been a pitcher for the Dodgers.

For the most part, we enjoyed indulging Christian's passion for baseball, but there were days when we prayed for relief from his tyranny. When he was in the role of pitcher, he begged us to run the bases each time a ball was hit, and he kept track of the score in his head. It was impossible to end our family baseball games until he was satisfied that the last out had been made. On one of our numerous outings to play baseball at a local high school, Christian spotted a metal cleat lying on top of a trash can in the dugout. This dirty, metal cleat became his most prized possession, and many nights he fell asleep cradling it in his arms.

One night before dozing off Christian said, "In the old days, we wore metal cleats but no batting helmets." This turned out to be yet another statement that proved to be true of baseball during Lou Gehrig's era. I discovered that metal cleats were invented in 1882, and batting helmets were not introduced in the Major Leagues until the mid-1950s. Christian was still three years away from being able to read when he said this and I was quite sure that he had never been exposed to this information.

Shortly before the release of Adam Sandler's movie *That's My Boy*, we received an e-mail from a reporter at the *Ventura County Star* by the name of Rhiannon Potkey. Rhiannon had been assigned the task of writing a light-hearted human-interest story about Christian being discovered on YouTube for the movie. However, it was clear from our e-mail correspondence that she was much more interested in Christian's obvious love of baseball than she was in his minor acting role. It was a Monday afternoon in May when Rhiannon showed up at our home to conduct the interview. Rhiannon's knowledge of sports—all sports—was way beyond my comprehension.

By asking a few questions, I found out that Rhiannon was once an accomplished athlete and had faced Serena Williams in more than one championship match during her days as a player in the fiercely competitive Southern California junior tennis circuit. Donning a bowl-cut hairstyle, she'd also battled it out on the Little League fields to earn her credibility among the boys, long before the notorious exploits of Mo'ne Davis in the Little League World Series. Unfortunately Rhiannon's athletic career was stunted due to debilitating pain, sometimes so extreme that she had to stay in bed for days on end and had to rely on friends to bring her food. She had warned me prior to her visit that if it was a bad pain day we might have to reschedule, but today was a good day.

When Rhiannon arrived, Christian was engaged in his normal ritual of playing baseball in our family room while Charlotte was in the kitchen preparing Kool-Aid for her upcoming seventh birthday party. I explained to Rhiannon that this was something Christian did every day for hours on end. The athletic news reporter jumped into the action right away, tossing balls to Christian and egging him on as he belted line drives off the microwave and hit pop flies into the ceiling fan. Rhiannon skillfully assumed the roles of pitcher and catcher in Christian's imaginary baseball game, while managing to simultaneously ask questions and jot down notes without getting hit by a single ball.

When the inquisitive reporter politely asked for my permission to interview Charlotte to get a quote about her brother, I willingly obliged. Rhiannon started by asking Charlotte why her brother liked baseball so much. This is when my worst nightmare became a reality. Charlotte's Kool-Aid-fueled monologue on Christian's past-life memories began with, "Christian used to be a tall baseball player. He played first base for the Yankees." Before I could interrupt, Charlotte had already spilled the beans. "He was Lou Gehrig, and he hates Babe Ruth."

I tripped over my words while attempting to explain to Rhiannon what Charlotte was talking about and then begged, "Would it be okay if we keep this off the record?" When she responded by laughing rather than the affirmative yes I was hoping for, I had visions of a headline that read: "Three-Year-Old Boy Thinks He Was Lou Gehrig." I was a nervous wreck just thinking about it.

In an effort to change the subject, I suggested we go upstairs so that Christian could give Rhiannon a tour of his room. As we passed the laundry room, Christian pointed out a pile of baseball pants with fresh grass stains and proudly said, "Those are my baseball pants." Rhiannon acted impressed when he added, "I made the green spots by sliding in the grass." She laughed when I told her Christian easily went through an average of 10 pairs of baseball pants per week and sometimes even managed to sneak his protective baseball cup to preschool without me noticing. The tour of Christian's room included an introduction to his beloved metal cleat, and he nearly burst with excitement when he showed Rhiannon his autographed ball from Matt Kemp.

As I walked Rhiannon out to her car, she said, "You remind me of Kathy Bryan, the mother of the Bryan Brothers." I knew exactly who she was talking about, not only because Kathy's twin sons were the most accomplished doubles team in professional tennis at the time, but also because I was a big fan of Kathy's husband, Wayne Bryan's, book, *Raising Your Child to Be a Champion in Athletics, Arts, and Academics*. I considered Kathy Bryan to be a role model, as a coach and as a parent, because she was an advocate for keeping sports fun for kids while instilling the values of hard work and discipline. Wayne Bryan's advice for parents and coaches was to never force a child to play against their will and to always keep them wanting more. Before departing Rhiannon said, "To say Christian eats, sleeps, and breathes baseball might be an understatement."

Michael was mortified when I gave him the news that Charlotte had told the reporter about Christian's claims of being Lou Gehrig. Michael huffed, "Great. The whole world is going to think our kid is nuts!" When the article hit the newsstands, two color photos of Christian graced the front page of the *Ventura County Star* below the giant headline, "Passion Never Off Base." Above the headline appeared a quote from me that read, "The kid is really lucky, but he has no idea. He just loves baseball." Rhiannon gave numerous examples of Christian's extreme baseball obsession and wrote of his baseball skills: "The left-hander has nearly perfect form when he swings a bat and an intense stare when he fires a pitch with a leg kick."

The article ended with a quote from Christian in response to why he never wants to stop swinging a bat or throwing a ball.

"Because I like baseball and I want to play it all the time."

Thankfully there was no mention of Christian claiming to be Lou Gehrig in a previous life. Rhiannon gave a fun description of Charlotte ducking to avoid balls as she made Kool-Aid during Christian's indoor batting practice. Charlotte's quote in the article was, "He always does this. He even does it at lunch." Michael and I were elated to have dodged that bullet.

CHAPTER NINE

TAKE ME OUT
TO THE BALL GAME

"I bleed Dodger blue and when I die,
I'm going to the big Dodger in the sky."

TOMMY LASORDA

That summer we celebrated the conclusion of the school year with a big seventh birthday party for Charlotte at our community pool, followed by a family reunion in Lake Tahoe. Our trip was actually a week-long 70th birthday celebration for my mom, her identical twin sister, and their best friend from high school. This was a trip I looked forward to taking every five years with my extended family because many of my fondest memories were created at this picturesque lake in the Sierra Nevada mountains. Although the people in our tightly knit group were all Southern California natives, we had gradually become more scattered throughout the United States as my generation settled down to have children of our own.

Our rendezvous at this sacred spot with my cousins and longtime family friends was like a walk back in time.

Seeing our children learn to water ski and skip rocks on this crystal-clear lake, just as we had done together in the 1970s, was surreal; a little slice of Heaven on Earth. Our time together at this alpine retreat also provided a perfect opportunity for me to discuss Christian's claims of being a baseball player in another lifetime with my three cousins, who were more like sisters to me. I told them how his storytelling had begun exactly a year before at our church camp in the woods when Christian was two years old. It was a pleasant surprise when my cousin Leanne, who owns a yoga studio in Nashville, was willing to entertain the possibility that Christian's stories were not pure fantasy. Leanne was promptly added to my short list of confidantes, which also included Michael, my mom, and Cinthia.

When we returned home from Lake Tahoe, I noticed a considerable change in Christian. On days when we attended Dodger games, he was much less inclined to talk about his past-life memories. Being immersed in the action of the Dodgers seemed to bring him into the present. Instead of wanting to talk about Babe Ruth and Lou Gehrig before bed, he preferred to rehash the Dodger game he had just watched and flip through the player photos in the Dodger media guide. This prompted my decision to take Charlotte and Christian to Dodger games multiple times per week that summer. My desire to get Christian out of the past and into the present was the prime motivation behind our frequent trips to the ballpark.

Dodger Stadium became our new Disneyland of sorts, with an equally colorful cast of characters we looked forward to seeing at every game. Michael's enthusiasm for making the long haul to downtown Los Angeles to watch the Dodger games was waning, so my friend Cinthia gladly scooped up his season ticket. She was a tremendous help when it came to keeping an eye on Charlotte and Christian at Dodger Stadium.

Dodger Stadium, commonly referred to as Chavez Ravine because of the narrow gorge in which the stadium sits, is the third-oldest ballpark in Major League Baseball and the largest MLB stadium by its seating capacity of 56,000. In the summer of 2012, Dodger game attendance was quite low, despite efforts by the new ownership group to boost the sagging fan morale left behind by the former Dodgers owner, Frank McCourt. This meant there were plenty of open seats right next to the Dodger dugout for us to choose from. This is where we met the colorful cast of characters who became our surrogate family.

There was Ernest the ice-cream vendor, who had been walking the Dodger Stadium aisles with his tasty treats for 50 years, and the friendly ushers who welcomed us with open arms to the front row seats, even though they knew our season ticket seats were way up in the nosebleed section. Charlotte and Christian acquired a deep respect for the always helpful police officers who lined the halls of the stadium and made them feel safe. There was also the full-time crew of landscapers who made sure that the lush turf was perfectly groomed before each game. The head groundskeeper, Eric Hanson, once said of the Dodger Stadium turf, "You can see there's a lot of science to it, but there's a lot more art." The combination of art and science he described struck me as very similar to the game of baseball itself. And then there were the Dodgers fans; the heart and soul of any Major League Baseball club.

Our newly acquired Dodgers family was quite diverse, but the one thing they all had in common was the fact that they bled Dodger blue, a phrase coined by longtime

Dodgers skipper Tommy Lasorda. At 84 years old, Tommy Lasorda was an honorary figurehead for the Dodgers and could be found at every home game, mingling with fans and never hesitating to sign an autograph or kiss a baby.

Leading our crew in the Dodgers cheering section was Hiccups the Clown, a Hispanic man in his late 20s who dressed up as a Dodger clown for every game, complete with face paint, a bulbous blue nose, big clown shoes, and a Dodgers jersey. We were first attracted to Hiccups because of the appealing photo opportunity and because of the way he made people smile. However, as we got to know the man behind the clown suit, it was his great big heart that we all fell in love with.

Hiccups was a real-life superhero, a man on a mission to feed the homeless and bring joy to the hospital rooms of pediatric cancer patients. In addition to his full-time job at a local children's hospital where he dressed up as a Dodgers clown on his lunch breaks to visit the kids who were being treated for cancer, Hiccups also rallied hundreds of people to bring pizza and clothing to homeless people on skid row in downtown Los Angeles once a month. In the midst of his already full life, our pal Hiccups managed to squeeze in taking care of his 99-year-old grandmother and attending nearly every Dodgers home game.

Our next friendship was formed when a friendly, upbeat Dodgers fan in his mid-50s noticed Christian's intense love of the game. This nice man named Russell had probably attended more baseball games in his life than most professional baseball players. Russell was as well-known at Dodger Stadium for his motto, "No bad days," as he was for his bright, Hawaiian-print, baseball-themed dress shirts. At times when I was unable to tear Christian away from the game to go to the concession stand or bathroom with Charlotte and me, Russell stood on guard until I returned.

Our little tribe expanded when we met Don and Merry, a fun-loving couple in their 70s who never missed a game, and then again when we met Rhonda, a kindhearted, Jewish mother of two college-aged daughters. Rhonda, who had recently beaten cancer, had more energy than all of us combined. She gave each member of our unofficial Dodgers fan club a necklace that said "Stay Positive," and we wore them at every game with pride. We were a motley crew of misfits who somehow fit together perfectly.

Charlotte and Christian never tired of singing "Take Me Out to the Ball Game" during the seventh-inning stretch or chasing the beach balls that inevitably bounced through the crowd whenever there was a break in the action on the field. They both knew the words to the national anthem by heart and had committed the names and numbers of their favorite Dodgers players to memory. Christian was completely enamored with left-handed pitcher Clayton Kershaw. When Clayton was on the mound, nothing could distract Christian's attention. After watching Clayton pitch in person at Dodger Stadium, our baseball-obsessed son would rush to the television to watch the replay of the game as soon as we arrived home. Christian studied Clayton's unique stretch and windup with laser-beam focus and practiced the 24-year-old-pitching-icon's movements over and over again, until he was able to imitate him perfectly.

I didn't think Christian's admiration for Clayton could get any greater, but my mind was changed when I witnessed him meet his larger-than-life hero in person at a fan appreciation event known as On-Field Photo Day. This is a tradition at Dodger Stadium that started in the 1970s where players mingle with fans on the field prior to a late afternoon game. Legions of fans gather around waist-high temporary fences while the players make their way around the penned-in area to pose for photos. Three-year-old Christian was awestruck when he saw Clayton making his way down the long line of adoring fans and stopping to pose for pictures.

When Clayton finally appeared in front of where we were standing, Christian was so excited that he completely froze. In an effort to break the ice, I handed Clayton the front page of *The Malibu Times* with the funny headline that read, "Watch Your Back Clayton Kershaw." Clayton laughed and said, "I've heard of this kid. A friend of mine sent me an article about him." I correctly guessed that Clayton was referring to Rhiannon's article in the *Ventura County Star* where Christian was quoted as saying Clayton was his favorite player. Clayton posed for a quick picture before continuing to make his way through the crowd.

After witnessing Clayton's generous spirit that day, I was curious to learn more about him. Online, I found the nonprofit foundation Kershaw's Challenge, which was created by Clayton and his wife, Ellen, to serve parent-less children in the most impoverished areas of southern Africa. In addition to donating $100 each time Clayton successfully struck out a batter, this young couple had also written a faith-based book called *Arise: Live Out Your Faith and Dreams on Whatever Field You Find Yourself* and had used the proceeds to build an orphanage in Zambia. Clayton and Ellen Kershaw had an obvious passion for helping others, and Clayton appeared to be a role model in more ways than one.

When I read that the Kershaws were planning a Texas hoedown barbecue-themed event at Dodger Stadium later that summer to raise funds for Kershaw's Challenge, I reached out to Ellen Kershaw to offer my services as a volunteer, given my fund-raising and event-planning background. My offer to help was well received, as Ellen was fairly new to Los Angeles and this was their first time putting on a fund-raiser of this magnitude. I called upon the help of my friend Cinthia, and the two of us spent the month of July rounding up sponsors and collecting donations to be auctioned off at the event.

Ellen and Clayton's charity event, held in a tent in the parking lot of Dodger Stadium, was a huge success. The highlight for Christian was pitching tennis balls to Dodgers catcher A. J. Ellis while Clayton looked on. When A. J. pretended that Christian's pitch had hurt his hand, Clayton said, "That's gas!" and gave Christian a high five. It was Clayton Kershaw's request to the Dodgers marketing executives to have Christian throw a ceremonial first pitch that ultimately sealed the deal. Thanks to Clayton's prodding, a young kid was granted the opportunity to throw a ceremonial first pitch for the first time in history. Christian would officially be making his big debut on the mound at Dodger Stadium in a few short weeks.

CHAPTER TEN

THE PITCH

"Any baseball is beautiful. No other small package comes
as close to the ideal design and utility. It is a perfect
object for a man's hand. Pick it up and it instantly suggests
its purpose; it is meant to be thrown a considerable
distance—thrown hard and with precision."

ROGER ANGELL

The school year commenced with Charlotte losing a
tooth on her first day of first grade and Christian throwing the ceremonial first pitch at Dodger Stadium on his
first day of preschool. By the time this day arrived, Christian could not have been more excited or better prepared
for his big moment on the mound. He had been practicing his imitation of Clayton Kershaw's unique stretch and
windup day and night. Charlotte and Christian slept the
entire way to Dodger Stadium while Michael and I did our
best not to think about all the things that could possibly
go wrong in the next few hours. In between our worrying,
we fielded calls from our friends and family who were en
route to meet us at the Dodgers game. When we arrived a
vivacious Dodgers employee greeted us at the main office

and escorted us past the tight security and onto the field, where the Dodgers were taking batting practice.

We had witnessed this pregame ritual many times from the stands, but this was Christian's first time experiencing it from the other side of the wall. Music filled the air as the players took turns batting from the netted batting cage at home plate. While the Major League players were launching home runs into the stands, Christian was behind home plate, hitting foam balls with his tiny wooden bat. He was thrilled when one of his favorite players, Andre Ethier, came over to shake his hand. The Dodgers outfielder made an even bigger impression when he peeled the tape off his hand to show Christian the blisters that had prevented him from taking batting practice that day.

Charlotte had given Christian a giant baseball for his fourth birthday just a few days prior, and he had brought it onto the field for his Dodgers heroes to sign. The look on his face was priceless when Dodgers manager Don Mattingly crouched down to sign the ball and pose for a photo with him. Coach Mattingly and Christian became fast friends in that moment on the field. I didn't know at the time that Don Mattingly had spent his entire MLB playing career, which had spanned from 1982 to 1995, as a left-handed first baseman for the New York Yankees, just like Lou Gehrig.

The stadium buzzed with excitement as the steady flow of people filled up the stands. The pregame crowd was larger than normal because the first 30,000 fans to enter the stadium would receive a Matt Kemp jersey, the promotional giveaway of the night. With the minutes remaining until game time steadily clicking down, it was time for our little pitcher to warm up his arm. I served as Christian's catcher while Dodgers legend Maury Wills stood behind him and offered pointers. In between pitches I glanced up at the stands and spotted my ex-boss, Magic Johnson, settling into his seat beside Tommy Lasorda near the Dodgers dugout. This was my cue that the pregame pomp and circumstance was about to begin.

My nerves were at an all-time high when the announcer asked the crowd to rise for the singing of the national anthem. As "The Star-Spangled Banner" rang throughout the stadium, I could hardly believe that the moment we had been waiting for was about to happen. When the music stopped, the video on the big screen cut to Christian smiling and waving while the announcer said:

> Ladies and gentleman, here to throw out tonight's ceremonial first pitch we have three-year-old Christian Haupt. He was discovered on YouTube by Adam Sandler for a baseball-playing cameo role in *That's My Boy*. He is a lefty and his favorite player is Clayton Kershaw. Christian lives in Westlake Village and is a Dodgers season-ticket holder. Today was his first day of preschool. Fans, please welcome Christian Haupt!

That was Christian's cue to take the mound. As he jogged away from the camera, the big screen showed Clayton Kershaw warming up in the Dodgers bullpen in the same white Dodgers uniform that Christian was wearing. Our son was oddly comfortable under the spotlight of the 30,000 fans in attendance. He confidently took his spot on the mound and cracked a smile as he leaned forward and put the ball behind his back. Pretending to shake off the catcher's sign, Christian slowly shook his head up and down, side to side, and then up and down again. He stretched his arms into the air above his head like his hero Clayton Kershaw, and then hurled the ball with all his might. The roar of the crowd took my breath away as the Dodgers catcher Tim Federowicz scooped up the pitch and jogged to the mound to greet Christian for a photo.

I wondered if Christian had noticed in all the excitement that the announcer who introduced him had mistakenly said he was three years old, unaware he had celebrated his fourth birthday just a few days earlier. As we were exiting the field to go to our seats, Christian wandered down the stairs of the Dodgers dugout and received a fist bump from Don Mattingly. As soon as we joined our friends and family in the stands, we heard the unmistakable voice of Hall of Fame Dodgers broadcaster Vin Scully over the loudspeaker. I had never been so happy to hear him say the words, "It's time for Dodger Baseball!"

The following morning I was flooded with voice mails and text messages from friends who had seen the photo of Christian's first pitch plastered all over the Internet. The Associated Press (AP) photo of Christian's first pitch taken by Mark J. Terrill was featured in the FOX Sports top photos of the day, and the photo received over 50,000 likes on the MLB Facebook page by 10 A.M. The YouTube video we posted of Christian's first pitch immediately went viral, but thankfully our son was completely oblivious to all the attention he was getting online. The FOX Sports article written by Joe McDonnell captured the moment best.

Three-year-old a film star, pitching prodigy

LOS ANGELES—On the warm night of Sept. 4, 2012, Christian Haupt stood on the mound at Dodger Stadium in his home Dodger whites, ready to throw the first pitch.

The lefthander—who models his style after Clayton Kershaw—stepped onto the rubber, looked in at catcher Tim Federowicz, nodded yes to the sign and threw. The pennant-race crowd went crazy—even though the ball bounced well short of home plate. Federowicz jogged out to the plate, giving Christian a high five as Haupt walked off the mound—and the crowd's ovation got even louder.

By now you're probably wondering why thousands of fans would cheer a bounced pitch so loudly—especially in the middle of a tight playoff race. Guess you had to be there.

Christian Haupt is just 3 years old. That's not a typo. He's really just three. And with the perfect motion—at least for a prodigy—he threw the ball harder, straighter and longer than most of the men, women or children chosen to throw out the ceremonial first pitch over the course of a season in Chavez Ravine.

CHAPTER ELEVEN

A NATIONAL TREASURE

"The foundation of life is love and respect."

Tommy Lasorda

While waiting for the Dodgers to return from their five-month winter break, Christian watched recordings of last season's Dodgers games over and over again. He still insisted on wearing a full baseball uniform and playing baseball for multiple hours every day, but somewhere along the way he had stopped asking us to call him Baseball Konrad. One evening before bed, Christian made a comment that made me think my plan to distract him from talking about his life as a baseball player during the early 1900s was working. He exclaimed, "I don't want to be an old guy anymore. I want to be a new guy like Matt Kemp (the Dodger outfielder)." I was overjoyed to hear these words come out of his mouth because it felt like a step in the right direction.

During the off-season, Christian invested so many hours into staring at the player photos in the Dodgers media guide that he even knew the names and numbers of the Minor League Baseball players by heart. When I heard the Dodgers were hosting a preseason FanFest in the parking lot at Dodger Stadium, I jumped on the opportunity to reunite Christian with his heroes. Apparently the 20,000 fans who showed up at the event were just as excited as Christian for the return of the Dodgers. He had a big grin on his face as he strolled down the blue carpet into the carnival-like FanFest. Once we passed through the entrance, we instantly became one with a massive sea of people dressed in blue and white. After trying every imaginable interactive baseball game, Christian grew tired of waiting in the long lines and asked if we could leave the FanFest to hit balls in the parking lot. The idea of being in a vacant parking lot away from the crowds sounded quite appealing, so I willingly obliged.

We found an open space outside of the FanFest where I could pitch to him without worrying about the foam balls hitting parked cars or people passing by. Each time Christian launched a ball into the air off of his tiny wooden bat, he made his customary victory lap around the imaginary bases. When he was in baseball mode, there was no stopping him. His serious demeanor made it look as if he had come here to work, not play. We repeated this drill for nearly an hour before a familiar face appeared behind the chain-link fence from inside of the FanFest. I was shocked and amazed when Baseball Hall of Fame Dodgers manager Tommy Lasorda called out to Christian, "What's your name, son?"

Without interrupting the flow of his game, Christian replied, "I'm Christian."

"You sure love baseball, don't you?" Tommy said.

Christian smacked a ball into the air with his bat and yelled, "Yep!" as he took off for first base.

Tommy instructed his assistant to fetch him a pizza, and he planted himself at a table near the fence so he could continue watching Christian's animated display in the deserted parking lot. When Tommy finished eating, he walked outside of the chain-link fence to offer some hands-on batting instruction. This gentle-natured 85-year-old man with an obvious love for children seemed nothing like the pop culture icon who had famously screamed at umpires during his 21-year career as the Dodgers skipper from 1976 to 1996. Tommy Lasorda turned out to be the exact opposite of the image I had in my mind for so many years before meeting him face-to-face.

Michael and I had attended an event a couple of years prior, a tribute to Sparky Anderson at California Lutheran University, where Tommy Lasorda had wooed the crowd with his dynamic storytelling. Each story had ended with a punch line that had left us laughing so hard we could barely breathe. Although I'm not sure Tommy was joking when he said he wants to have the Dodgers schedule placed on his grave so people can check it to see if the Dodgers are playing at home or on the road when visiting their loved ones at the cemetery.

My favorite story of the night was when Tommy talked about how he had tried to cheer up his losing team by telling them that the best team in all of baseball, the 1927 Yankees, had lost nine games in a row, and the Dodgers had only lost seven games in a row. Tommy went on to say the Dodgers won 10 games in a row after that speech. When Tommy's wife asked him if the 1927 Yankees had really lost nine in a row, he replied, "How the hell do I know? That's the year I was born. It sure sounded good to those guys though." I love this story because, in addition to showing Tommy's hilarious sense of humor, it also illustrates his belief that success doesn't necessarily come from being the best, but from believing you're the best.

Here in a vacant parking lot, the former Dodgers manager was busy coaching a four-year-old while thousands of Dodgers fans were roaming around on the opposite side of the fence. As Christian smacked the balls, Tommy yelled out, "Chop that tree!" and "Take a ride on that one! It would cost you ten dollars in a taxi to go that far!"

I hoped that Christian would remember this moment when he was old enough to realize how special it was. Before going our separate ways, Tommy reached out his hand to Christian and said with authority, "Let me see a nice, firm handshake, son. We always look a person in the eye when we shake their hand. A smile goes a long way too." Tommy then signed a baseball with the inscription, "To Christian, a future Dodger." When I later heard from a Dodgers employee that Tommy frequently signs this inscription to kids, it only made the ball more special. It was Tommy Lasorda's creative way of instilling the belief that anything is possible with hard work and determination.

When I left my business card with Tommy, I never imagined I would receive a call from him a few days later. I was helping out with Charlotte's softball practice when the voice mail from Tommy came in.

"Cathy, Tommy Lasorda. I'd like to talk to you about— I'd like to film your little guy swinging that bat. That's an amazing, amazing thing for a young man like that to swing the bat the way he does, and I'd like to have it on file, on film. Is that okay with you?"

I returned the call right away, and Tommy subsequently invited Christian to attend Dodgers spring training in Arizona the following week.

A few days later, we packed our car and embarked on the six-hour drive to Phoenix, Arizona. I had heard of spring training before, but I had no idea, until we arrived, just what we were in for. This month-long series of exhibition games and practices is a ritual that began in the 1890s in Hot Springs, Arkansas, where players convene to shake off the dust and prepare for the upcoming 162-game season. Baseball fans from all over the country now flock to spring training facilities in Arizona and Florida during the month of March to watch the 30 Major League Baseball teams face off in friendly competition. When I called Tommy Lasorda to let him know that we were in town, he told me we were in for a treat. Tommy had been participating in this annual tradition for more than 60 years.

Tommy requested that we meet him at the Dodgers training facility at Camelback Ranch in Glendale, Arizona, the following morning. When we arrived at the baseball complex, it was easy to spot Tommy by the long line of people waiting for his autograph. He sat at a table with his assistant and signed autograph after autograph for the fans while Frank Sinatra music played on his old-style, portable boom box. When he saw us in the crowd, he signaled for us to come over. Tommy affectionately put his arm around Christian and asked, "Are you ready to play some ball today?" Christian nodded and whispered yes under his breath, but he looked as nervous talking to Tommy as I remembered him being the last time he had sat on Santa's lap. Tommy said, "Come on back in about thirty minutes, and we'll go play some ball with the Dodgers." A big smile lit up Christian's face. Now Tommy was speaking his language.

Christian and I headed to a grassy area to play catch while we waited for Tommy to finish his autograph-signing session. Before we knew it, Tommy drove up in his golf cart and asked us to hop in. With Tommy as pilot and Christian as co-pilot, they looked like twins. Tommy was decked out in his pristine, white Dodgers uniform from head to toe for the first day of spring training, and Christian was wearing his standard Dodgers whites as well. Tommy drove us through the security gate and onto the field where the Dodgers players were warming up for batting practice.

Tommy waited until he had the undivided attention of the Dodgers players, and then he directed the Dodgers videographer to film Christian hitting foam balls with his little wooden bat. Christian sent a ball flying into the air.

"He hit that one good," Tommy said, then to Christian, "You hit a home run on that one." After a few more good whacks of bat on ball, Tommy said to Christian, "Okay, now let me see you pitch." Christian gave him his standard line whenever it was time to stop hitting:

"Okay, one more hit."

When Christian finally set down his bat and put on his glove, the videographer shot footage of him pitching and catching fly balls as Tommy looked on with rapt attention. He said to a Dodgers pitcher standing nearby, "The kid throws heat." Christian had the time of his life playing baseball in the company of his Dodgers heroes, and they seemed to get a kick out of Tommy Lasorda having them watch a four-year-old play baseball in the middle of their spring training camp.

The following morning when we stopped by Tommy's autograph-signing table, he gave Christian the pep talk of a lifetime. Tommy reached his arm around Christian.

"Remember all that work you did yesterday?"

Christian nodded.

"One day, do you want to play for the Dodgers?"

When Christian answered yes, Tommy gently said, "You could because you can hit that ball, and you can catch that ball, and you can run. But how bad do you want it? That's what really matters. Do you really want it?"

Listening intently, Christian had a very serious look on his face when he nodded his head yes.

"It isn't always the fastest man who wins the race or the strongest man who wins the fight," Tommy continued. "It's the one who wants it more than the other guy. If you want to play for the Dodgers badly enough, and you're willing to put in the work, you can do it."

Then, out of the blue, Christian said to Tommy, "You used to play for the Yankees."

"Yes, son, I was with the Yankees organization for one year."

I was astonished when Tommy confirmed that he had indeed played for the Yankees. This is not something Christian could have known, and I didn't even know it myself. I later discovered that Tommy's brief stint with the Yankees as a left-handed pitcher hadn't even made it into his Wikipedia bio.

This shift in the conversation provided a perfect opportunity for me to hint about Christian's stories of being a baseball player in the 1920s and '30s. I was curious to see what Tommy would have to say about it. I gently eased into the topic.

"Christian is a big fan of Lou Gehrig. Did you ever see Lou Gehrig play?"

Tommy leaned down to Christian.

"Oh, you picked a good one," he said in a soft voice, "one of the best. He was my hero when I was a kid."

Christian listened intently.

"He was a good man—the hardest working man in baseball."

Now I jumped in.

"Christian has been telling us that he used to be Lou Gehrig since he was three," I told Tommy. "He told us things he could have never known at the time, like, 'I used to stay in hotels nearly every night' and 'I rode on trains.'"

Tommy smiled and said, "The kid's got a good imagination."

This wasn't exactly the response I was hoping for, but I didn't have the nerve to explain further. I still wasn't sure what to make of Christian's past-life claims myself, but I had come to the conclusion that some things in life do not need to be fully understood in order to be appreciated.

Tommy put his hand on Christian's shoulder.

"When I was fifteen years old, I used to actually dream I was pitching in Yankee Stadium. Bill Dickey was my catcher, and Lou Gehrig was my first baseman. Then years later, in my real life, they called me to pitch to Yogi Berra. There I was, warming up in the bullpen in Yankee Stadium. I said I'd been here many times, but in my dreams."

Tommy patted Christian on the back.

"Never stop dreaming, son."

CHAPTER TWELVE

I JUST KNOW

"I see great things in baseball. It's our game—the American game. It will take our people out-of-doors, fill them with oxygen, give them a larger physical stoicism. Tend to relieve us from being a nervous, dyspeptic set. Repair these losses, and be a blessing to us."

WALT WHITMAN

The next time we crossed paths with Tommy Lasorda was a month later when I took the day off of work and surprised Charlotte and Christian by letting them skip school to attend Opening Day at Dodger Stadium. I picked up Cinthia at 10 A.M. in an effort to beat the traffic jam that would inevitably result from 56,000 people racing to get into the stadium before the opening pitch at 1 P.M. We made our way through the crowd and to our seats just in time for the pregame festivities. Patriotism filled the air as jets flew overhead and hundreds of military servicemen and servicewomen in uniform unfurled a billowing American flag across the field.

Following the national anthem, Magic Johnson emerged from the dugout, and the crowd roared as he walked toward the mound with a ball in his hand. Just as

Magic started his windup to toss the ceremonial first pitch, he was interrupted. Dodgers manager Don Mattingly ran out on the field with one of the greatest pitchers of all time to relieve Magic of the duty. The fans went wild when legendary left-handed pitcher Sandy Koufax pitched a perfect strike.

Then the real game began and Christian was elated to see Clayton Kershaw take the mound. Clayton hit his first career home run that afternoon and made it into the baseball record books by being one of only two players in history to ever pitch a complete-game shutout and hit a home run on Opening Day. The crowd celebrated their home team's 4–0 victory over the rivaled Giants as Randy Newman's iconic 80s song "I Love L.A." blared throughout the stadium. I found myself so immersed in the excitement of the game that it was hard to imagine my life before baseball.

After the game we met up with Tommy Lasorda in the Dodger Stadium Dugout Club. This is when we received the news that the award-winning photo of Christian's first pitch, taken by AP photographer Mark J. Terrill, was now hanging in the private Owners' Suite at Dodger Stadium. An executive from Magic Johnson Enterprises, who was also in the Dugout Club after the game, told us he had been in the Owners' Suite earlier that day when Sandy Koufax had seen the framed photo of Christian hanging on the wall. He said Sandy had loved the photo so much that the Dodgers owners had offered to send one to his home. Tommy gave me, Christian, Charlotte, and Cinthia a legendary Lasorda hug before heading to his car.

We later found out that the photo of Christian's first pitch was also hanging in the Dodgers Stadium Club and in the lobby of the Guggenheim Partners' headquarters in Chicago. The photo of Christian's first pitch had been selected as a top photo of the year in 2012 by *The Atlantic* magazine, ESPN, and FOX Sports, but we never imagined it would show up on the walls of Dodger Stadium or in the home of Sandy Koufax. Christian was one lucky four-year-old.

Michael and I were still completely exhausted by Christian's relentless pleas to play baseball with him day in and day out, so we sought revenge by signing him up to play baseball in two different baseball leagues that spring, which he absolutely loved. Between Charlotte's softball schedule and Christian's baseball schedule, we found ourselves at a grassy field nearly every day of the week. Christian's appetite for playing baseball was like that of a border collie playing fetch—enough was never enough. After playing baseball outside for hours, he played inside of our house, throwing tennis balls against the walls and hitting foam balls over our second-story banister until it was time for him to go to bed.

To capture this special moment in time, Michael and I created a video montage of the many creative ways Christian had discovered to play baseball within the confines of our home, and uploaded it to YouTube. Much to our surprise, the video became an instant hit and garnered millions of views. Thankfully the casualties from Christian's indoor baseball practice were limited to small holes in the drywall that were easily repaired, cracked glass in our picture frames, and numerous drinking glasses caught in the line of fire. We learned to stop using our expensive glasses after Christian's line drive shattered Michael's favorite crystal wine glass. Without missing a beat, Christian said, "Daddy, you can't make friends with a wine glass. Just grab a new one."

The fields where Christian played baseball were the same fields where I had played softball as a kid in the 1970s. Although I never had any conscious desire to be a baseball mom, the joy of being a parent in the stands far exceeded my wildest expectations. My initiation into the sisterhood of baseball moms had occurred a year earlier when Christian was hitting balls with his tiny wooden bat at the Honolulu airport while we were waiting to board our flight.

A friendly woman approached me and reminisced, "I remember those days. When my son was a toddler, he used to take rolled-up socks from my laundry basket and throw them against the wall to practice pitching. Now he is the first baseman for the New York Mets." She proudly pulled out her son Ike Davis's MLB card from her wallet and said, "Enjoy every moment! There's no better place to build character than a Little League baseball field."

I never imagined at the time that this quintessential American pastime would be such a blessing in our lives. There was something about moments spent on the Little League baseball fields that eased everyday worries and made it seem as if all was well in the world. The Little League pledge, which was written in 1954, sums up the principles at the heart of Little League baseball: "I trust in God. I love my country and will respect its laws. I will play fair and strive to win. But win or lose, I will always do my best."

Following the regular season, Christian was invited to play on a travel baseball team made up of five- and six-year-old boys with an equal love of the game. The majority of our weekends were spent at baseball tournaments where these young boys poured their hearts and souls into playing up to five games over the course of two days.

Our habit of attending Sunday morning church services became increasingly sporadic as baseball took over our lives. My weekend mornings now started with a ritual of packing up the car with all of the essentials for our long, hot days under the sun. While the boys played as many as three baseball games per day, Charlotte and the other siblings kept themselves entertained by making rainbow loom bracelets in the stands.

The world of travel baseball united families of all different ages, races, religions, and socioeconomic backgrounds. We developed an undeniable sense of camaraderie through our time spent together in the trenches. The barriers that may have existed between us in more formal settings didn't exist here, and long-lasting friendships were forged on and off the field.

Michael made quite an impression on our travel baseball team at our parents versus kids scrimmage. First, because he had no idea how to catch with a baseball glove, and second, because he didn't realize he was supposed to drop the bat after hitting the ball. When Michael was called "out" for running all the way to second base with a bat in his hand, he argued in his German accent, "How was I supposed to know that?" The kids and parents broke out in uncontrollable laughter when it became obvious that Michael was not joking. After this embarrassing moment, he promptly bought himself a baseball glove, and Christian taught him how to catch with it. I was thrilled to be relieved of some of my baseball duties when Michael mastered our new pitching machine and started playing baseball with Christian in our front yard. He also spent countless hours hitting tennis balls to Christian with a tennis racquet for fly-ball practice—the diving catches were Christian's all-time favorite.

In the midst of travel ball season, Christian's bedtime storytelling ritual about his life as Lou Gehrig resumed without warning. However, this time he expressed his feelings about Lou Gehrig and Babe Ruth with a surprisingly mature perspective. What Christian had shown through raw emotional reactions to Babe Ruth as a toddler, he now talked about with a deeper understanding of the emotional context. One night before bed, Christian said out of the blue, "Babe Ruth was a very jealous man." When I asked him why Babe Ruth was jealous, he immediately replied, "Because he was not related to Lou Gehrig's mom." This made no sense to me at the time, but it did inspire me to resume my late-night investigations into the life of Lou Gehrig.

My research revealed that Babe Ruth and Lou Gehrig, who had been the best of friends since 1925, vowed never to speak again after a falling-out between Lou's mother and Babe in 1932. Prior to making this statement about Babe Ruth being jealous, Christian had no way of knowing that the feud between Lou Gehrig and Babe Ruth had originally stemmed from a disagreement between Babe Ruth and Lou's mother, Christina Gehrig. I read that Christina had become like a surrogate mother to Babe Ruth, who had been raised in an orphanage and didn't have a mother of his own. It was written that Babe spoke German with Lou's mother and loved her German cooking. By 1927 Babe Ruth had become a fixture at the Gehrig home, where Lou still lived with his parents.

When Babe remarried in 1929, he began leaving his 11-year-old daughter from a previous marriage in the care of Christina Gehrig while he and his wife, Claire, traveled. When Lou's mother told Babe and Claire she felt they were neglecting his daughter, it was the end of the relationship between Babe Ruth and the Gehrig family. I read an article that said Babe sent his Yankees teammate Sammy Byrd to deliver the following message to Lou: "Never speak to me again off the field." As legend has it, the two men never acknowledged each other from that day forward. The fact that Christian was able to explain the emotional context of the feud between Babe Ruth and Lou Gehrig, without ever being exposed to this information, just blew me away.

Christian looked at a photograph of Babe Ruth and Lou Gehrig standing together.

"Even though Lou Gehrig and Babe Ruth played baseball together and took pictures together," he said to me, "they didn't talk to each other." It was a statement right out of the baseball history books, but Christian still didn't know how to read, and there was no reasonable explanation as to how he would know such a thing.

When I asked him how he knew, he replied, "I just know."

Christian continued to offer up new details about Lou Gehrig's life with astounding accuracy, but he now spoke about Lou Gehrig in the third person, rather than speaking in the first person. For example, where Christian used to say things like, "I stayed in hotels and rode on trains," he now said, "Lou stayed in hotels and rode on trains."

During my research I stumbled upon a radio interview from 1939, in which Lou Gehrig named young Ted Williams out of Minnesota as a promising up-and-coming player in the Major Leagues. This was the same Ted Williams from the photograph that Christian had persuaded me to purchase for him at Fenway Park when he was two years old. As fate would have it, Ted Williams made his Major League debut against the Yankees on April 20, 1939. This was the only game in which Lou Gehrig and

Ted Williams ever played against each other because Lou announced his retirement from baseball shortly thereafter.

An even stranger discovery I made that summer was when I noticed the remarkable resemblance in Christian and Lou Gehrig's hitting mechanics. When I showed Michael a YouTube video of Christian's first baseball tournament, and we compared it to videos of Lou Gehrig playing baseball, he agreed that the similarity was undeniable. Christian and Lou both stood at the plate with their front elbow fully extended, rather than slightly bent like the majority of batters. We also noted a similarity in the unique way that both Christian and Lou Gehrig slid into the bases with one arm up in the air and one arm dragging behind them.

Watching the YouTube video of Christian's first baseball tournament, we noticed for the first time that Christian removed his batting helmet right after scoring a run and waved it in the air, much like Lou Gehrig's customary tip of his hat to the crowd after hitting a home run. All the other kids in the video removed their helmets *after* walking into the dugout. Although Lou Gehrig was once a top pitcher at Columbia University, there didn't appear to be any surviving video footage of Lou pitching on YouTube, so we were never able to compare their pitching mechanics.

For Christian's fifth birthday in August 2013, I made arrangements for him to throw a ceremonial first pitch at a Minor League Baseball Reno Aces game while we were visiting friends in Lake Tahoe. There was nothing Christian enjoyed more than fraternizing with the "big" baseball players. Despite the fact that he had come down with a bad cough due to wildfires in the nearby Tahoe National Forest, Christian trotted out to the pitcher's mound and gave it his all. After the first pitch, we practically had to drag Christian away from his new pal, Reno Aces' manager Brett Butler, who also happened to be an ex-Dodger and fellow lefty. The Aces were up by three runs at the top of the third inning when Michael and I noticed that Christian's breathing was becoming increasingly labored. The combination of the high altitude and smoke from the wildfires was more than his fragile lungs could handle.

My good friend Mela, who lived nearby, offered to take Michael and Charlotte to the Circus-Circus Hotel and Casino for a much-needed distraction while I drove Christian to the emergency room at Saint Mary's Regional Medical Center. Watching our son gasp for breath and seeing his heart practically beating out of his chest at what felt like a hummingbird's pace was something I had grown accustomed to over the past five years. Yet it still broke my heart every single time. Christian clung to me with fear in his eyes as the ER doctor injected him with steroids to treat his breathing difficulties. When he was finally stabilized and released from the emergency room, I vowed to do whatever I could to keep this from happening again.

The following day I flashed back to Carol Bowman's book, *Children's Past Lives*, and the e-mail she had sent me. Carol had suggested in her e-mail that Christian's breathing ailment could be related to Lou Gehrig's tragic death from ALS. I was alarmed to discover the most common cause of death among people with ALS is respiratory failure. I recalled Dr. Ian Stevenson from the University of Virginia School of Medicine having a similar theory.

Dr. Stevenson's research had revealed that the majority of cases of children who remember past lives involve a premature death from unnatural causes in the previous lifetime. Carol Bowman took the scientific data a step further by suggesting the spontaneous appearance of past-life memories in childhood could be the soul's way of resolving "unfinished business" from the previous lifetime. She believed that simply acknowledging children's past-life memories could provide healing and closure. Even though the idea of a physical ailment being caused by a tragic death in a previous lifetime struck me as completely irrational, I was willing to consider anything that might provide healing for our son. I had already exhausted every rational treatment for Christian's asthma under the guidance of the top pediatric pulmonary doctors in Southern California.

The combination of Christian's asthma attack and the resurgence of his past-life memories had created the perfect storm. It inspired me to seek the expert advice of Dr. Jim Tucker, the current Director of the Division of Perceptual Studies at the University of Virginia School of Medicine founded by Dr. Ian Stevenson in 1967. I was delighted when Dr. Tucker offered to make the trip to California to meet our family.

CHAPTER THIRTEEN

THE GOOD DOCTOR COMES TO TOWN

"Dust thou art, to dust returnest
Was not spoken of the soul."

HENRY WADSWORTH LONGFELLOW

As recently as two years ago, the skeptic in me would have been appalled by the mention of "reincarnation" or "parapsychology," yet today I jumped out of bed eagerly anticipating the arrival of the leading researcher in the field. Perhaps today would be the day when Michael and I would finally receive answers to the questions that had been plaguing us for the past two and a half years.

Jim B. Tucker, M.D., an associate professor of Psychiatry and Neurobehavioral Sciences at the University of Virginia School of Medicine was our greatest hope for a reasonable explanation as to what was going on with our son. We were still recovering from the trauma of our pastor insinuating that Christian was possessed by the spirit of a dead person. My initial inquiry to Dr. Tucker a few months prior had really been a plea for help in our quest to understand our five-year-old son's peculiar behaviors.

When Dr. Tucker's book *Return to Life: Extraordinary Cases of Children Who Remember Past Lives* was released in 2013, I devoured it from cover to cover in two days. It is a straightforward, analytical account of several cases that Dr. Tucker had personally investigated using the strict scientific methodology instituted by his predecessor, Dr. Stevenson. Dr. Tucker's goal in each case was to determine what the child had said, how the parents had reacted, whether the child's statements matched the life of a particular deceased person, and whether the child could have acquired the information through normal means—such as books, movies, or overheard conversations.

Reading about other American children with parents like us, who did not believe in reincarnation before their own personal experiences, is what inspired me to send Dr. Tucker an e-mail outlining Christian's odd statements and behaviors. The fact that the families featured in Dr. Tucker's book had the option of changing their names to protect their identity eased our apprehensions about having Dr. Tucker come to our home to interview Christian. The last thing we wanted was to destroy our son's life by having kids on the playground or baseball fields find out about our family secret.

Jim told us there was somewhat of an urgency to his visit because Christian was approaching the age when the memories and associated behaviors start to fade for the majority of children who recall previous lives. I was a little worried that we had already missed the window that Dr. Tucker was referring to because Christian had recently said before falling asleep, "It's hard to remember when I was a tall baseball player because God gave me a new brain now." The vivid images he had shared with us were becoming foggy in his mind in a way I imagine must have felt like trying to grasp the details of a dream as they drift away into oblivion.

Dr. Tucker, who prefers to be called Jim, knocked on our door at 9 A.M. on Wednesday, April 2, 2014, as promised. He had flown into Los Angeles the night before and would fly back to Virginia after our meeting. Christian bounced his way to the front door but waited for me to open it. His hesitance was partially due to the latch we had installed at the top of the door, which was still above his grasp, but primarily because he was nervous about meeting Dr. Tucker. Under normal circumstances, he would have grabbed a chair from the dining room to open the door for himself. We were greeted by a soft-spoken man with a generous smile and a subtle Southern accent left over from his childhood days in North Carolina, where he was raised as a Southern Baptist.

When Michael returned from dropping off Charlotte at school, he shook hands with Jim and excused himself to his makeshift office in our dining room. Even though he was just as curious about Dr. Tucker's evaluation of our son as I was, Michael liked to pretend that this "past-life thing" was mine, not his. Behind the scenes both Michael and I found solace in the fact that Jim had come from a religious background similar to our own. In a strange way, it made us feel less guilty about entertaining the idea that our son had lived before.

Jim arrived with a handwritten spreadsheet of Christian's statements, which he had extrapolated from our e-mail exchanges leading up to his visit. He was very methodical, scientific, and gentle in his approach, in a Mister Rogers sort of way. After getting acquainted Jim suggested we play a little baseball out in front of our house to put Christian at ease. Jim threw on a baseball glove for a game of catch, and before long the three of us were in a full-fledged baseball game in the middle of our street. Christian barely noticed that Jim was interviewing him as I ran the bases and they tried to get me out.

"What did your mother cook for you when you were a tall baseball player?" Jim asked.

"She knows," Christian pointed at me, "because she was my mom when I was Lou Gehrig."

It was slightly awkward because I hadn't told Dr. Tucker about Christian saying that I was his mother in his previous life, but he didn't appear surprised by the remark. It was a conversation that would have seemed bizarre to anyone but Jim, who was well versed in the subject.

As somewhat expected Christian was shy about talking to a stranger about his past life as Lou Gehrig. Every time Christian had spoken about being a tall baseball player in a previous life, it had been right before falling asleep at night or just after waking up. I figured the odds of uncovering any new information at this time of day would be slim. Dr. Tucker had told me that he never expects to reveal new information in an interview setting because spontaneous recollections of a past life can't be forced on the spot. He had also said many of the children in the cases that he and Ian Stevenson studied spoke about their past-life memories when they were drowsy. Despite the fact that Christian was far from drowsy, Jim continued to ask him questions after we moved our outdoor baseball game into the living room. Then came a question I found disconcerting.

"Do you remember how you died?" Jim asked Christian.

I'd never asked Christian about dying before, so this was brand-new territory for me. Christian's response shocked me even more than Jim's question. In a matter-of-fact tone, Christian replied:

"My body stopped working, and I didn't feel anything."

"Then what happened?" Jim asked.

Christian threw a tennis ball against the wall above our staircase, dove across the floor to catch it, and replied, "After I died, I became Christian."

Christian threw another ball, dashed over to the landing to retrieve it, and then said out of the blue, "I picked her to be my mom, and then she got old."

"When did you pick her?" Jim asked calmly.

"When she was born."

"Do you remember where you were when you picked her?"

Without hesitation Christian said, "In the sky."

I was trying my best to stay calm through all this and now, I had a question too.

"What happened between the time you picked me to be your mother and the time when you were born and I was 'old'?"

He shrugged his shoulders and said, "I don't know. I don't remember."

Just when I was starting to think Christian was making the whole thing up, Jim stunned me by saying, "The memories children report of the time between lives often seem very incomplete, but many children in the cases we've studied do recall choosing their parents." Jim went on to say that Christian's response that he was "in the sky" was consistent with reports from other children who had claimed to have chosen their parents before being born. This unexpected revelation gave me a brand-new perspective on life and death. It was the first time I had considered the possibility that we choose to be born and even have a hand in selecting our parents.

While Christian continued his indoor baseball routine, Jim and I excused ourselves to discuss the more esoteric concepts from his book, such as quantum physics and the role of the soul in human consciousness.

"You can think of the human body as a radio," Dr. Tucker said. He clapped his hands together as if simulating an explosion and said, "If you smash the radio, it loses the ability to play any music. However, this does not mean that the radio waves have disappeared. There's just nothing to receive them."

"Aha! So when a body dies, the soul still exists in a form that we can't see?"

Jim nodded. "Precisely!"

I told Jim that I was particularly intrigued by a case he had described in his book, *Return to Life*, of a young boy who had specific memories of being the legendary golfer Bobby Jones in a previous lifetime. This case study hit home with me because this seven-year-old golf prodigy had told his parents at the age of three that he had been Bobby Jones when he was "big." The boy further surprised his parents when he provided historically accurate details about the life of Bobby Jones, which he had never been exposed to, much like Christian's revelations about the life of Lou Gehrig. This child also showed a proficiency at golf that was far beyond his years, winning 41 out of 50 junior golf tournaments at the age of seven while competing against kids who were much older. The other uncanny similarity was the fact that Lou Gehrig and Bobby Jones—born in 1903 and 1902 respectively—had both suffered crippling health conditions that had led to their untimely deaths.

I knew from reading Dr. Tucker's book that, for their research purposes, the University of Virginia's Division of Perceptual Studies does not generally consider cases of children purporting to have been famous people because there is a higher probability of the child obtaining the information through books, movies, or overheard conversations. Dr. Tucker said that the combination of this young golfer's reported memories coupled with his prodigious talent for golf is what led him to accept the case as valid past-life remembrance, despite the fact that Bobby Jones was a famous person.

Michael and I had never considered Christian to be a prodigy in the traditional sense of the word, but he did seem to come into the world with a type of "remembering." In his theory of reminiscence, Plato asserted that "knowledge easily acquired is that which the enduring self had in an earlier life, so that it flows back easily." I told Dr. Tucker about a theory I had come across from Edgar Cayce, the renowned Christian mystic, that many child prodigies with a talent beyond their years are born with a conscious recollection of this ability that had been developed in a previous life. I told him I had read that Cayce found it particularly true in cases where a child is born into a family with no affinity for the expressed talent, such as George Frideric Handel, who displayed early musical talent and became a skillful musician, despite the fact that he had been strictly forbidden by his parents to play any musical instrument. Jim told me that his mentor, Dr. Ian Stevenson, had come across many children in his studies who displayed skills that seemed to be carried over from a previous life. I wasn't totally ready to ascribe Christian's early baseball skills to a past life, but it was starting to seem like a plausible explanation.

As Dr. Tucker packed up his briefcase, I seized the moment to tell Jim about the angel Lailah from the Babylonian Talmud and how she extinguishes the memories of the soul before birth by pressing upon the child's lip and saying "shhh."

"I like to think that the angel Lailah just didn't press quite hard enough on some children's lips," I told Jim, "so they come into this life bearing soul memories from a previous lifetime."

Jim then shared the story of the River of Forgetfulness from Plato's *The Republic*. Dr. Tucker said many ancient Greeks believed that souls were made to drink from the River of Forgetfulness before being reincarnated so that they would not remember their past lives.

"This amnesia serves a purpose because it allows the individual to embark on the new life unencumbered by echoes of the past," he said.

I asked Jim if he had any theory as to why the majority of children who remember past lives recall lives of individuals who died at a young age.

"Dying young in a previous life increases the likelihood that a child will come into the world with memories of the prior lifetime." Among the University of Virginia's 2,500-plus documented cases of children who remember past lives, the median age of death in the previous life is 28 years old. Dr. Tucker explained, "The endings of the past lives tend to be like dreams that end prematurely."

He said the best analogy to describe what is happening with these children is to imagine that they are being abruptly woken up in the middle of a dream and then quickly falling back asleep to continue the same dream in the next lifetime. Dr. Tucker believes emotional connections or unresolved emotional issues may affect where the individual comes back in the dream, or in the next lifetime.

"It is quite common for a child to return to the same family if there are strong or unresolved emotional connections to family members from the previous life," he explained. "In same-family cases, it appears the children come back to the same dream to continue the story with their families, in a different role."

The most promising element of Dr. Tucker's book, *Return to Life*, was that in every single case, there came a time when the child's past-life memories ceased. When I brought up this topic with Jim, he said, "We often see the associated behaviors fade as well around the time the child reaches six or seven, eight at the latest."

His words gave me hope to cling to. I longed for the day when Christian would say to me the words a child in Jim's book had said to his mother, "Mommy, I just want to be me, not the old me." Christian had shown progress in that regard when he'd said he wanted to be a "new guy like Matt Kemp," but he wasn't quite there yet.

Before departing Jim honored my request to sign my copy of his book, and the inscription read: *Cathy, thank you for sharing Christian's story with me.*

I thanked Jim for making the trip, and Michael took a break from his computer to say good-bye. After giving Jim a departing hug of appreciation and encouraging Christian to do the same, I said:

"I find your scientific approach to the subject of reincarnation comforting because it doesn't feel unorthodox and New-Agey like the past-life regressions I've read about where people go under hypnosis to access past-life memories."

Jim surprised me by saying, "Most of the time hypnotic regression seems to produce fantasy, but there are a
few rare cases where people came up with accurate information from the past that's very hard to explain."

Hearing this tiny bit of optimism toward past-life
regressions from someone whom I considered to be a
highly intelligent and rational person made me wonder.
Should I give this past-life regression thing a try? My mind was
still reeling from Christian's new revelation that he had
chosen me to be his mother when I was born and from
Jim's confirmation that many children who recall past
lives also remember choosing their parents. A longtime
friend of mine named Tracy had been encouraging me to
do a past-life regression ever since I had told her about
Christian insisting that I was his mother when he was Lou
Gehrig, but I had never seriously considered doing it until
this moment.

That night I playfully asked Christian as I was putting
him to bed, "Do people get to choose if they want to come
back as a person or an animal?"

With a big smile he replied, "Of course not, Mommy!
God decides that. You *do* get to pick your parents."

Christian's next comment really made me think. He
said with certainty, "It's not a talking situation, though,
because there are no words there."

CHAPTER FOURTEEN

I WILL FIND YOU

"Don't be dismayed at good-byes. A farewell is necessary
before you can meet again. And meeting again, after
moments or lifetimes, is certain for those who are friends."

RICHARD BACH

Dr. Tucker's words about children claiming to have
chosen their parents prior to being born stuck with me
and inspired me to call my good friend Tracy for advice.
Tracy was my go-to person for all matters in the woo-woo
zone. She and her husband, Jeff, were among my most
trusted confidants when it came to the subject of Christian's reported past-life memories. Over the course of our
15-year friendship, Tracy had spent her free time practicing yoga, meditating, and handcrafting beaded jewelry,
while I was busy running marathons, working overtime,
and juggling social commitments. The fact that we were
polar opposites created an attractive force that had kept
our friendship going strong over the years. While I had
always been a master at keeping my mind and body in perpetual motion, as if taking a moment to slow down would
lead to my certain demise, Tracy was a seeker of peace and
tranquility. She relied on intuition where I required cold,

hard facts. Tracy also happened to hold the distinction of being the only person in my life who even knew what a past-life regression was. Not only did she know what it was, she had actually experienced one before.

When I called Tracy to say that I was opening up to the idea of undergoing a past-life regression, she couldn't have been more surprised. I had made it pretty clear to her in our previous conversations that I considered hypnotic regression to be the equivalent of going to a fortune-teller or a psychic—a big *shall not* in the Bible. Not only was it in direct conflict with my Christian beliefs but it also struck me as complete nonsense. When Tracy had first suggested the idea of having me visit her friend Jeroen, my skepticism outweighed my curiosity. It wasn't until I heard Christian say he had picked me to be his mother that I actually considered acting on Tracy's suggestion to contact Jeroen.

Sensing that I was finally ready to take the leap, Tracy gently prodded, "If you decide to do a regression, you should definitley do it with Jeroen. He is a good person, and I trust him." After swapping numerous voice mails with Jeroen, I became well acquainted with his Dutch accent and successfully arranged an appointment for the following Wednesday at 10:30 A.M.

The day started like any other Wednesday morning— waking up at 5 A.M. to ride my stationary bike for 60 minutes, checking e-mails, taking a quick shower, packing lunches, getting my kids fed, bathed, and out the door by 8:15, followed by 45 minutes of volunteering in Christian's kindergarten class. Without telling Michael where I was headed or what I was up to, I embarked on my journey to a suburb near downtown Los Angeles to meet the man known on Instagram as "Jeroen Is Love." I figured it would be best to wait to tell Michael about my little adventure until I knew exactly what I was getting myself into.

To say I was nervous when I knocked on the door of past-life regression therapist Jeroen de Wit would be an understatement. Even though I had skipped my morning coffee, as recommended in the four-page list of pre-session guidelines, my heart was beating faster than normal. Because the guidelines indicated that the session could take up to five hours and would require some recovery time, I had cleared my day of appointments—other than a Dodger game with my family that evening. The exact words in the document were: *You will feel as if you have returned from an amazing journey, having visited other lifetimes, and it is best to give yourself some time to fully return to your regular conscious day-to-day reality before attempting any complex mental tasks or strenuous physical activity.* Even though I didn't really believe it, I went along with the charade.

After a knock on the door, I was greeted by a sweet-tempered man with a broad smile, deep dimples, and twinkling blue eyes that appeared to light up from within. Jeroen lived on the top level of a home, which was built into a hill, and ran his Source Energy Healing business out of the bottom floor. He invited me into the downstairs room, which was sparsely decorated with a couple of chairs and a large massage table—the table where I was possibly going to surrender my consciousness. At that moment I wished I had scheduled a massage instead. Little did I know that I was about to embark on the most riveting journey of hypnotic time travel imaginable.

I scanned the room for clues about the man who would soon guide me into a trance using Dolores Cannon's Quantum Healing Hypnosis Technique (QHHT).

Stunning nature photographs, shot by Jeroen, adorned the walls, and the room exuded the same warmth as its owner. Jeroen invited me to sit down, and his black-and-white cat took it as a cue to cruise up the back stairs.

"I don't normally do things like this . . ." were the first words out of my mouth, as if I was confessing a sin. He listened patiently as I went into a lengthy dissertation on the reason for my visit and my desire to better understand Christian's journey.

Then he said, "It's important to have an open mind and to release expectations you have about the lifetime that you would like to visit. It's impossible to predict what lifetime your subconscious mind will choose to explore." Our pre-session conversation turned into more of a therapy session as I revealed how the whole experience with Christian and his connection to Lou Gehrig had me questioning the tenets of the faith I'd grown up with. Jeroen's lightness of being gently loosened the screws of my tightly wound resistance, and by the end of our discussion, I felt quite comfortable that I was in good hands.

Jeroen wrapped up our pre-session consultation by saying, "Don't worry about trying to remember what you are seeing, hearing, or saying because I'll be providing you with an audio recording of our session together." He lit a small bundle of sage and waved the smoky mass around the room and then around me. Although I didn't know the exact purpose of this ritual, I figured it couldn't hurt. I followed Jeroen's recommendation to go to the bathroom because he said I would most likely be in a state of hypnotic trance for a few hours. And then I cautiously climbed onto the massage table and closed my eyes.

After the hypnotic induction, Jeroen gently asked, "Where are you?"

Two-year-old Christian in his favorite baseball attire.

Adam Sandler and two-year-old Christian on the set of *That's My Boy* in August 2011.

A family portrait with cousins in spring 2011 *(karenhalbert photography)*

Christian filming the baseball scene for the movie
That's My Boy in Cape Cod, Massachusetts.

Cathy, Michael, Charlotte, and
Christian in Hawaii in fall 2011.

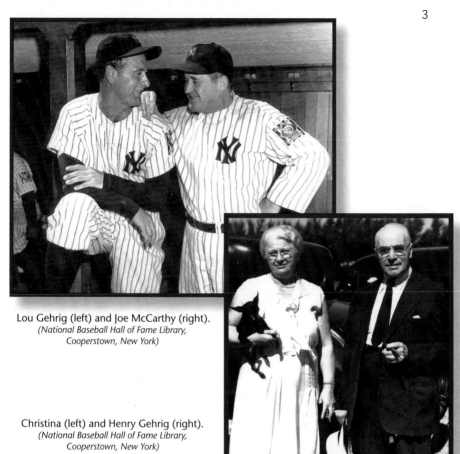

Lou Gehrig (left) and Joe McCarthy (right).
*(National Baseball Hall of Fame Library,
Cooperstown, New York)*

Christina (left) and Henry Gehrig (right).
*(National Baseball Hall of Fame Library,
Cooperstown, New York)*

1927 Yankees team photo, Lou Gehrig in back row on far left.
(National Baseball Hall of Fame Library, Cooperstown, New York)

Christian at Dodger
Stadium in spring 2012.

Three-year-old Christian warming up for
his ceremonial first pitch at Pepperdine
University in May 2012. *(Ed Lobenhofer)*

Christian (left) meets Dodgers outfielder
Andre Ethier (right) at Dodger Stadium
On-Field Photo Day 2012.

Charlotte at Dodger Stadium
in August 2012.

Christian at Dodgers batting practice prior to his ceremonial
first pitch on September 4, 2012. *(Ed Lobenhofer)*

Christian throws the ceremonial first pitch at Dodger Stadium
on September 4, 2012. *(AP Photo/Mark J. Terrill)*

Christian's ceremonial first pitch at Dodger Stadium
(Photo by Jon SooHoo/Los Angeles Dodgers, LLC)

Christian imitates Dodgers
pitcher Clayton Kershaw's
stretch. *(Ed Lobenhofer)*

Christian (right) with Dodgers manager
and former Yankees first baseman Don
Mattingly (left). *(Ed Lobenhofer)*

National Baseball Hall of Fame manager
Tommy Lasorda (left) and Christian (right)
at Dodgers spring training 2013.

7

A ball from Tommy Lasorda inscribed:
To Christian, a future Dodger.

Tommy Lasorda gives pointers to four-year-old Christian
at Dodgers spring training in Glendale, Arizona.

Christian sleeping with baseballs he collected at Dodgers spring training.

A typical week's worth of Christian's dirty baseball pants.

Cathy (left) and four-year-old Christian at the Dodger Stadium Club in 2013. *(Charlotte Haupt)*

Christian (left) and Charlotte (right)
at Dodger Stadium.

Christian (left) meets legendary Dodgers
broadcaster Vin Scully (right).

Cathy, Christian, Michael, Charlotte, and family pets in 2013.
(Peter Lars © Cornerstone)

10

Dr. Jim Tucker from the University of Virginia School of Medicine (left) interviews five-year-old Christian (right) about his past-life memories while playing baseball in April 2014.

Christian shooting the FOX Sports MLB All-Star Game Pregame Show in June 2014.

Cathy wearing the required white gloves while viewing documents at the National Baseball Hall of Fame Giamatti Research Center in July 2014.

Lou Gehrig.
(National Baseball Hall of Fame Library, Cooperstown, New York)

Christian (left) and Charlotte (right) visit Lou Gehrig's former home at 9 Meadow Lane in New Rochelle, New York.

Lou Gehrig and his mother, Christina Gehrig.

Cathy (left) and Christian (right) at Lou Gehrig's former home.
(Charlotte Haupt)

Christian visits Lou Gehrig's graveside in New York.

Christina "Mom" Gehrig (center) with Ellsworth Hawkins (left)
and Ralph P. Clarkson (right) at Lou Gehrig Memorial Little
League Field dedication in Milford, Connecticut, in 1952.
(Courtesy of Ken Hawkins)

Six-year-old Christian on the field at Dodger Stadium
with Dodgers first baseman Adrian Gonzalez.
(Photo by Jon SooHoo/Los Angeles Dodgers, LLC)

Little League Opening Day 2015. Cathy (top row center) and Christian (bottom row second from left). *(Ultimate Exposures)*

Six-year-old Christian on the Little League pitching mound.

Tommy Lasorda (left) and Christian (right) at Little League Opening Day 2015.

From left: Christian, Reverend Ken Steigler, Cathy, Charlotte, and Marilyn Steigler (seated) in New Hampshire. *(Lori Dickman)*

Cathy (left) and Christian (right) win Lou Gehrig photo in Tampa Bay, Florida in July 2016.

Christian at Cooperstown Baseball Camp in July 2015.

Eight-year-old Christian on the pitching mound in September 2016.
(Photography by Michael Coons)

Images slowly started flooding into my mind. What started out as a bird's-eye view of a busy suburban neighborhood with trees, came closer into focus, until I found myself standing in front of an iron stove in the kitchen of what I described as my "not fancy" apartment.

"What does it feel like?" Jeroen asked.

"I just get a feeling of being a mother. I keep being drawn to the kitchen." He instructed me to look at my hand, and I giggled as I described it as "white and pudgy."

Lying on the table with my eyes closed, I had the sensation of being in another body, a weighty one. I described feeling "weight in my face, weight in my stomach, in my arms." At the same time, my logical mind was totally coherent and questioning the validity of the words flowing out of my mouth. It almost felt as if I was two people at the same time—this person in the heavy body I was describing, as well as a skeptical observer. Even more bizarre was that I was speaking in a voice I could barely recognize as my own, using words and grammar that sounded totally different than my regular vernacular. When Jeroen prompted me to look at my feet, I gazed past my long dress and apron and clearly saw myself wearing big, heavy, brown boots, which I said were "for working."

"Do you live with any other people in the house?" Jeroen asked.

"Two men—a boy and a man." I described them sitting at a table and said, "The man seems like, not engaged. Just kind of doing his own thing."

"How do you feel about the boy?"

I felt a flood of happiness, my face barely able to contain my big smile.

"The boy, I love."

I told him what I saw in my mind's eye: the boy was wearing boots, high socks, a hat, and pants that went to his knees. I added, "He's handsome. He is probably like nine years old or so."

"How does the boy call you?"

With a laugh, I replied, "Mama."

He then asked how the man addresses me, and I laughed even harder when saying, "Mama!" In that moment, my logical mind was chattering in the background, telling me there was no way that a man would call his wife "Mama." And yet, even as I doubted, the more sensations and almost visceral knowledge of this "other" life washed over me. (Against all odds exactly one year after this session with Jeroen, I came across a newspaper article from 1933 in which Lou Gehrig's father was quoted referring to his wife as "Mama.")

I told Jeroen that my husband spent most of his time at home and often smoked a pipe while sitting in the big, black chair in the living room next to "an old stove oven." When Jeroen asked about my little boy a second time, I felt myself beam with pride as I said, "He's a good boy."

"When you're hugging him, what do you tell him?"

I mumbled, "*Meine Liebe*? Like it's German . . . he likes to have fun and play—works hard." Jeroen's questioning narrowed down the location of our home to a suburb outside of New York, not near the water, where we traveled by trolley cars to go into the city. I playfully joked about wearing a lot of clothes, even on very hot days, because of wanting to cover up my heavy body.

Jeroen then said, "So let's leave this scene. On the count of three, you will be transported to the next important scene in this lifetime, whatever you consider to be important. One, two, three . . . what's happening now?"

In an instant I was transported to a big, grassy parking lot in front of a baseball stadium. He asked what we were wearing, and I said we were kind of dressed up. I described myself wearing a long, floral-print dress, closed-toe shoes, and a white hat with a big brim, and I said my husband was wearing a coat and hat for the occasion.

"What about your husband? How do you address him?"

Misunderstanding the question, I answered with a hearty laugh, "He just kind of wears the same thing all of the time. He just wears pants and a shirt and a belt."

Jeroen asked again, "How do you address him? How do you get his attention?"

"Heinrich," I replied.

He then asked what language we speak at home and I said, "German, Deutsch."

"Where is your boy?" Jeroen asked.

"He's playing in the game, so we're gonna watch him. He's new though." I said I was excited for him because he had always wanted to do that, even though I wished he would have finished school. Jeroen and I both chuckled when I said, "The baseball people came in. They got him." I explained how they had come to his college and watched him play, then I reiterated, "They got him!" When Jeroen asked if I was familiar with the game of baseball, I told him how my son and his friends had played baseball with wooden sticks as kids.

Each time Jeroen asked a question, I was treated to vivid 3-D imagery of what was happening around me, a high-definition virtual reality. He asked if we had special seats, and I said, "Kind of; not too close." I explained, "He's on first base, so when I sit on that side, I can see pretty good."

"And what team does he play on?"

"It's the Yankees," I replied, "they have on the short pants—like knickerbocker type pants."

When Jeroen asked me what the uniforms looked like I said my son was wearing a white, pinstripe jersey with the number four, while the other team was wearing red jerseys with short, gray pants. This is when my logical mind kicked into high gear. *Was I simply reciting information I had come across from my prior research on Lou Gehrig, describing images I had already seen?* After all, I knew from my hours and hours of research that Lou Gehrig wore the number four and played first base for the Yankees. Then I surprised myself when I began describing and experiencing things from totally out of the blue that I never could have known.

"Do you guys have any snacks while you're watching the game?" Jeroen asked.

"Yeah, we have these nuts. They cook these nuts that we can eat. They're pretty good." He asked if they brought them to our seats, and I responded that we had to "get 'em."

"Are you drinking anything?"

"Maybe a cola," I replied.

My use of the word *cola* came as a big shock to me, even under hypnosis, because it's not a word I had ever used before. I was completely dumbfounded when my later research revealed that roasted chestnuts were sold at the front entrance to Yankee Stadium and all dark-colored, carbonated beverages were described as "colas" at the time.

When he asked me what the scoreboard looked like, a crystal-clear view of it popped into my mind. I said it was a big, black sign in the distance with "numbers that have to be changed . . . like a person does it. It's not electric." Jeroen then had me fast-forward to the end of the game, and I heard the roar of the crowd, cheering for the win. I was beaming with pride when I said, "He hit one over the fence." Adding, "He's a gentleman. He's humble."

"Do you ever talk to the people who run the team or have contact with them?" Jeroen asked.

"Not too much. Some of the players visit sometimes. He lives at home."

"How old is your son?"

I blurted, "Twenty-two." (I later found out that even though Lou Gehrig was signed by the Yankees in 1923 at the age of 20, his first season playing for the Major League club was two years later when he was indeed 22 years old.) When Jeroen asked what we do after the game, I said we went to eat some food and drink a beer in the city. Our entire dialogue was in the present tense with me speaking in the first person as Lou Gehrig's mother. As I answered Jeroen's questions with my eyes closed, I could see the action unfolding in colorful moving pictures in my mind.

Jeroen guided me to leave this scene and move on to the next significant scene in the life of this woman. *Bam!* There I was back at Yankee Stadium, but this was a very different feeling because it was the day my son was retiring from baseball as the result of a medical issue. The sensations came rushing in. As I remarked that the loud popping sounds coming from the cameras were hurting my ears, I could actually feel the pain in my ears. I told Jeroen the loud noise might be coming from the flash, even though it was daytime, not nighttime. (I later read that flash photography was commonly used in daylight hours during the 1920s and '30s, and I was surprised to learn that the flash was created using an explosive powder so dangerous that the loud pyrotechnics led to the death and disfigurement of many professional photographers during this era.)

When Jeroen asked where we lived, I saw the home and described it as a "bigger house" that "sits on a hill," and said our son had bought it for us. In response to Jeroen's question about my son's age, I said he was now 39. (My later fact-checking revealed that Lou Gehrig was 36 years old when he gave his "Luckiest Man" speech on July 4, 1939.) I sounded distressed when I said, "His body is sick . . . He can't run. He can't hit . . . but he's still a gentleman."

"Do the doctors know what's going on with your son?"

"Not sure, not sure. But he'll be okay."

"So you're not too worried about it?"

With complete confidence I replied, "No. He's gonna be okay."

My logical mind was in total disagreement on this one because I knew that Lou Gehrig had died shortly after his retirement from the Yankees. But lying there on the table, I felt a mother's confidence that her son was going to be okay.

I told Jeroen my son was now married and described his wife as a "funny lady." I said, "She doesn't like to come to our house so he comes by himself."

"So when you say 'funny lady,' do you not like her?"

"She likes things her way."

I admitted to Jeroen that my son loved her, but added, "There were better ones." When Jeroen asked if they ever had kids, I replied, "Nope," and further explained, "I don't think she could have kids."

"At least they're happy together."

"Yeah, he's a good boy."

When Jeroen complimented me on the job I did raising my son, I happily accepted the compliment and said thank you. I was coherent enough to realize that our conversation was getting stranger by the second. I said my son's wife "didn't like too many people," but that my son liked *all* people. Except . . .

"He doesn't like Babe Ruth," I said.

"Why not? What happened?"

"It was bad. He was bad to Lou's wife. He tried to make moves to his wife."

This information didn't come as a complete surprise because I had prior knowledge of the feud between Babe Ruth and Lou Gehrig, but it felt quite strange to be experiencing the emotions firsthand from the perspective of Lou Gehrig's mother. Most remarkable was the roller coaster of emotions I felt while describing each scene. My emotions ran the gamut of sadness, excitement, pride, humor, joy, disbelief, and despair.

Jeroen then prompted me to move forward to the next significant day in the life of this woman, and I was propelled into a scene many years later.

"Now it's just me. No husband and no son," I said.

When Jeroen asked me how my son had died, the sadness I felt was gut-wrenching. I expressed having been very surprised by Lou's death.

"Was he seen by doctors?"

"Yeah, they couldn't do anything."

"Do they know what it was?"

"They think he had a problem with his nervous system. I don't know."

"Did you know it was coming or was it unexpected?"

"It was pretty quick. It's too bad he didn't have any kids," I said with a heavy heart.

I said my husband had a tough time after our son's death and drank a lot. I reported my husband's death to be the result of a heart attack.

Jeroen then guided me to go to the next significant scene in this lifetime. I immediately found myself lying on a hospital table.

"I think, like the doctors are working on my body."

"How old are you?"

I blurted, "Sixty-two." I said my body was going to be cremated and told him my memorial service was attended by "no family, mostly strangers." I then described feeling my soul slip out of a tired and worn-out body to be reunited with my family and a little dog in Heaven. Jeroen asked how my husband looked. I chuckled and made Jeroen laugh when I replied, "Better."

"Is Lou there?"

I nodded and my voice quivered as I described Lou coming toward me to give me a hug.

"Ask Lou, ask him why he needed to leave this lifetime so early."

I replied, "Why did you have to leave so early? Why did you leave me? He said, 'I chose this.'"

"Why did he choose it?"

"Lou said, 'Better to have lived.'"

"What else do you want to ask him?"

I asked, "Will I see you again?"

"What does he say?"

"I will find you," I said as tears started to roll down my cheeks.

"So what do you feel now?"

Smiling through the tears, I replied, "I feel like he did find me. In Christian, he did."

"He is Christian?"

"Yeah."

"So he kept his word?"

"Yeah," I replied now laughing through my tears, "Now what? What are we going to do?"

"It's okay, we'll find out."

Jeroen then asked for permission to talk to the subconscious of Cathy and began asking questions of my higher self. This is when our conversation shifted from the bizarre experience of me speaking in the first person as Lou Gehrig's mother to the even stranger phenomenon of speaking about myself in the third person.

"What was the purpose of this lifetime?"

"To heal, to feel complete," I responded with my eyes still closed.

"What was the purpose of Cathy and Lou being reunited in this lifetime?"

"Just completion . . . to relive the good times too," I said as a feeling of peace filled my entire body.

When I opened my eyes and saw Jeroen's face, it felt as if only minutes had passed. My first clue that a significant amount of time had gone by was that I already had an urgent need to go to the bathroom again. Before heading back home, I gave Jeroen a great, big hug; I felt a special bond with this man I had met only three hours earlier. In the hours and days that followed, I wondered, *Could the purpose of life on Earth really be that simple? Is it possible that we chose this life, as Christian had told Dr. Tucker, with the ultimate purpose of enjoying the good times together?*

CHAPTER FIFTEEN

A MOTHER'S LOVE

"Love bears all things, believes all things, hopes
all things, endures all things. Love never ends."

I CORINTIANS 13: 7-8

When I arrived home from my three-hour session
with Jeroen, I was still digesting what had just occurred
and not in the mood to discuss it with anybody. However,
while putting Christian to bed that night, I felt my eyes fill
with tears. I had to tell him something for the first time.

"I believe you. I was your mother when you were Lou
Gehrig."

Christian's eyes lit up, and I could tell he wanted to
hear more about my change of heart. When I told him
about my journey to the past and my peek into life as Lou
Gehrig's mother, he enthusiastically inquired, "Was it a
machine? Can I do it too?" I asked Christian if he remembered being married when he was Lou Gehrig, and his
response was not what you would expect to hear from a
five-year-old.

"She drank alcohol, and there was a lot of yelling, like
Babe Ruth." The last words out of his mouth before falling
asleep were, "Lou should have never married that dumb

lady. She was drunk." This was the last time I ever brought up the subject of Lou Gehrig's wife with Christian because it was obviously a sore subject.

Jeroen sent me the audio recording of our session the following day via e-mail, but I couldn't bring myself to listen to it because I was still coming to terms with the very strange feeling of literally walking in someone else's shoes and body. Besides, I didn't feel a need to listen to the recording because I could recall everything I had said under hypnosis perfectly. The vivid imagery of the scenes I had experienced were as fresh in my mind as if I had been there in person or seen them in a movie. I did, however, have a strong urge to scour the Internet for historical facts about Christina Gehrig's life to see if the details I had revealed during our session had any basis in reality.

When I discovered photographs that were eerily similar to the images I had seen in my imaginary movie, I excitedly texted them to Jeroen with captions such as, "Those are the shoes!" I sent him a photo of the old Yankee Stadium scoreboard from the 1920s and wrote, "The scoreboard really was manually operated!" Most shocking was my discovery that Lou Gehrig was 22 years old when he played his first season in the Major Leagues, just as I had reported while under hypnosis. Although Lou Gehrig was first signed by the Yankees a few days before his twentieth birthday, he did not make the Yankees' major league roster until replacing Wally Pipp as the starting first baseman two years later. This timeline is something I absolutely did not know prior to my session with Jeroen.

Ironically the old Yankee Stadium that I had seen so clearly during my past-life regression was torn down in 2008, the same year of Christian's birth, to make way for the ultramodern new Yankee Stadium. My fact-finding mission also led me to discover a home at 9 Meadow Lane in New Rochelle, New York, that Lou Gehrig bought for his parents in 1927. The modern-day photograph I found of 9 Meadow Lane looked very much like the home on top of a hill I had described living in at the time of Lou's retirement.

To my astonishment every statement from my past-life regression that was verifiable turned out to be historically accurate, with the exception of three key facts. I had erroneously reported that Christina Gehrig died at the age of 62, rather than 72, and I was three years off when I said Lou Gehrig's retirement speech took place when he was 39 years old. The third and most unsettling discrepancy of my past-life regression was my comment about being extremely surprised by my son's death. It wasn't just the comment but the feeling of certainty I had when saying he would be okay and the confusion I felt after he had died.

It appeared from my research that Lou Gehrig was aware of his imminent death prior to delivering his "Luckiest Man" speech at Yankee Stadium on July 4, 1939. If documented history was right, it would make sense that Lou Gehrig's parents also knew that he had very little time left to live. If this was in fact true, my comment under hypnosis about being surprised by Lou Gehrig's death must have been wrong. This inconsistency is what fueled my desire to take a deeper look into Christina Gehrig's life and death.

When my online search for the details surrounding Christina Gehrig's death came up empty, I ordered a copy of her death certificate from the Connecticut Public Health Department to see if my description of her dying in a hospital and being cremated was accurate. When I received the death certificate in the mail a couple of weeks later, I was blown away to read that she had indeed died in a hospital and her body was cremated, just as I had reported. I was finally convinced there was something greater than pure coincidence going on.

I became obsessed with researching the unique relationship between Lou Gehrig, his mother, and his wife. In the midst of busy work days, I would find my mind drifting to the topic of the Gehrig family. In between calls to my real estate clients or while waiting for a home inspection to be completed, I used my cell phone to search the Internet for clues. In an article written by Lou Gehrig shortly before his marriage in 1933, he wrote, "My mother is my inspiration, my sweetheart, my manager, my all. Around her revolve all of my activities." At 30 years old, Lou was still living with his parents, and it was reported that his mother could always be found in the stands at his games, both at Yankee Stadium and on the road.

All of that changed when Lou fell in love and married Eleanor Twitchell. A close Gehrig family friend, Fred Lieb, wrote about their tempestuous relationship in his book *Baseball As I Have Known It*. Fred's exact words were, "It would be nice to report that things thereafter were harmonious between Mom and her daughter-in-law. But from the start there were clashes whenever the elder and younger Gehrigs got together." Fred reported that the hostility between the two women remained unabated long after Lou's death. Considering the depth of animosity between Christina and Eleanor, I was intrigued by the subtle choice of words I had used to describe Eleanor while under hypnosis. I described Lou's wife as a "funny lady" who liked to control things. Reflecting upon this understated comment led me to believe that Lou's mother had a kind heart and was not one to speak ill of people—even people she wasn't fond of.

The greatest revelations about the Gehrig family feud came from a book co-authored by Lou's wife, Eleanor, entitled, *My Luke and I*. Eleanor wrote that Lou would sometimes get upset with her drinking because he wasn't a big drinker himself. She wrote about a particular incident that had occurred on a ship during a 1934 tour of the Orient with an all-star baseball team that had completely enraged Lou. According to Eleanor's own account, she went "missing" on the ship for two hours. Lou was livid when he found her in Babe Ruth's cabin, drinking champagne with Babe and his wife. This event cemented the feud between Lou and Babe that had started two years prior. What struck me most about this story was how it seemed consistent with Christian's comments about the drinking and yelling when I'd asked him if he remembered being married. I wondered if this could have also been the episode of Babe Ruth trying to "make moves" on Lou's wife that I spoke about during my past-life regression.

As I continued to unearth evidence consistent with the facts I had revealed under hypnosis, the chains of my skepticism were further loosened. I was convinced that something very real, beyond my understanding, had occurred while I was in a state of hypnotic trance, yet I wasn't sure why or what it all meant. *Was the information being channeled from some other dimension, or was it actually buried deep within the layers of my soul?*

CHAPTER SIXTEEN

LOVE NEVER DIES

"In music, in the sea, in a flower, in a leaf,
in an act of kindness . . . I see what
people call God in all these things."

PABLO CASALS

I now questioned the beliefs I had clung to for the past 40 years. I felt as if I was cheating on Jesus as I searched for answers, exploring different religions and examining the ancient scriptures they were founded upon. I was shocked to learn that even though only 25 to 30 percent of Americans believe in reincarnation, it is a majority belief among the collective population of the world. I found myself inspired by passages in the Jewish Talmud, the Christian Gnostic Gospels, the Islamic Quran, the Hindu Bhagavad Gita, and the Kabbalah, that explicitly express a belief in reincarnation. According to the Gnostic Scriptures, even Jesus spoke of "rebirth." My greatest discovery of all was the realization that at the root of all religions is a respect for a universal power greater than ourselves and a dictate to love one another.

My search into the history of reincarnation also led me to many prominent philosophers, poets, scientists, and thought leaders who accept the concept of reincarnation as an indisputable truth. I discovered through my research that the concept of reincarnation has been a recurring theme in literature, science, and religion since the beginning of recorded history. I was intrigued to learn that Plato, Socrates, Rumi, Voltaire, Carl Jung, William Wordsworth, Walt Whitman, Henry Wadsworth Longfellow, Edgar Allan Poe, W. B. Yeats, General George Patton, and Henry Ford were among the long list of believers in past lives and the probability of living more than one lifetime.

Goethe remarked at a friend's funeral, "I am certain that I have been here as I am now a thousand times before, and I hope to return a thousand times." Henry David Thoreau believed reincarnation to be a deeply rooted instinct of the human race and was among the many who have had a very strong sense of the déjà vu, the experience of "having been there before." Albert Einstein had this to say after the passing of his dear friend, "Now Besso has departed from this strange world a little ahead of me. That means nothing. People like us . . . know that the distinction between past, present and future is only a stubbornly persistent illusion."

I was especially moved by the teachings of the Dalai Lama, who preaches that inner tranquility comes from the development of love and compassion for ourselves and others. Tibetan Buddhism is a religion of kindness based upon the fundamental principle that caring for the happiness of others releases our fears and gives us the strength to cope with any obstacles we encounter. The Dalai Lama's teaching that the purpose of life is to pursue happiness and relieve suffering resonated with me more than ever after receiving the message during my past-life regression that Christian and I had chosen to come back for the simple purpose of reliving the good times. *Is it possible that the simple pleasures of life on Earth, like watching a baseball game, eating an ice-cream cone, swimming in the ocean, a warm embrace, or watching a sunset could be some of the reasons why we choose to come back?* Integrating this philosophy into my belief system made me treasure the "doing" a little more and treasure the "getting it done" a little less.

I believed the Dalai Lama when he said, "where there is true compassion, anger and hatred cannot exist." This tenet was not far from the biblical teachings I was raised with. However, when it comes to the topic of reincarnation, Christianity and Tibetan Buddhism do not see eye to eye. When I learned that that the concept of "rebirth" was prevalent in Christian scriptures and widely accepted by early church leaders, I gave myself permission to be a practicing Christian and believe in the possibility of living more than one lifetime.

Although believing in reincarnation is no longer a crime punishable by death, it is still a polarizing concept. When I looked into how and why the concept of "rebirth" was shunned by church leaders in the 4th century, it appeared to be a means of keeping the faithful obedient and loyal to the church and state. After experiencing the bizarre events that had recently transpired in my life, I could no longer deny the mysterious forces of the universe that connect us all. It became clear to me that the primary purpose of life on Earth is to learn how to love and honor one another in good times and in bad. Surrendering to the fact that no human being will ever have definitive answers to the mystery of life is what ultimately gave me peace of mind on the subject of reincarnation.

Then came the challenge of integrating the concepts of love and compassion into my daily life. After undergoing the past-life regression, I felt a palpable shift in my perspective. As I started to look at every human being as a soul with a body that could be taken off like an old shoe, I felt more compassion toward people in all walks of life. My heart began to open up like a flower in bloom, and as my armor was stripped away. I found myself being less judgmental of myself and others. Practicing yoga and meditation taught me that inner peace is a state of mind, which can only be achieved by going within. Michael was less than thrilled when I began going to a 4 A.M. Sadhana Meditation class, but I explained to him that meditation quieted my mind and allowed me to hear the whispers of my soul, much like prayer. Through a daily practice of prayer and meditation, I discovered that the subconscious mind is a gateway to the Divine.

However, I still found it challenging to practice the principles of love and compassion when it came to Little League baseball. In the spring of 2014, an opposing coach got wind of Christian's past-life stories from a mutual friend and began using this information to ridicule our son. In front of a group of Little League parents, he said, "That kid is crazy. He thinks he was Lou Gehrig." The moment I heard about this, my feelings toward this man were far from compassionate. I actually wanted to take him down—like a mother bear protecting her cub. Moments like this made me realize that I was far from being the enlightened Zen master I felt like during my morning mediation class.

I was clearly not alone in my struggle to behave humanely when it came to watching our kids play baseball, as evidenced by the countless times our games were delayed due to boisterous arguments among the coaches while the bewildered young boys wondered why everyone was so upset. It was not uncommon to witness coaches berating their players for striking out or making an error. I once saw a father scream to our team in the dugout, "We're not here to have fun, we're here to win." Such scenes were probably unfathomable to the founder of Little League baseball, Carl Stotz, whose vision in creating the league was to foster cooperation, teamwork, and respect for others. A mother in the stands said it best when she shouted to coaches who were arguing over an umpire's call, "Who cares about baseball, we're training young men here!"

In one of our Little League play-off games, the son of the coach who had ridiculed Christian did something that made my blood boil. By the first inning, I could feel myself getting upset when the opposing coach's seven-year-old son, who was playing first base, heckled the umpire. When the umpire called "ball one," the boy yelled out to his pitcher, "Don't worry about it, Jack. That umpire doesn't know what a strike looks like." I was most appalled by the fact that the boy's father did nothing to correct his son and appeared to condone the disrespectful comment.

And then two innings later, the same boy was up to bat and hit a ground ball to second base. The second baseman scooped up the ball and threw it to Christian at first base for an easy out. This is when the coach's son, who was two years older and much bigger than my son, ran out of the basepath to knock Christian down in an attempt to get him to drop the ball—a tactic this boy used quite frequently. Christian managed to hold on to the ball, but he was taken out of the game with a neck injury. I found myself wanting to ring the kid's neck and tell the father to jump off a cliff. No matter how much I tried to feel compassion and love for this coach, all I felt was rage.

The following day I sent an e-mail to the League requesting that a warning be issued to the boy prior to our championship game. By trying to single out the boy to get revenge on his father I was just as guilty of violating the principles that Little League baseball was founded upon as the coach whom I had come to dislike. I didn't like this side of myself, but my acrimonious feelings toward the coach seemed beyond my control. It became obvious to me that I still had a long way to go in my new spiritual practice of love, compassion, and forgiveness. My inside job was far from over, but I was slowly learning that only when the mind is quiet can the heart become open.

CHAPTER SEVENTEEN

WHISPERS
OF THE SOUL

"Put your ear down close to your soul and listen hard."

Anne Sexton

At the end of our Little League baseball season in June 2014, I indulged my ongoing curiosity about the life of Christina and Lou Gehrig by going to see Jeroen for another past-life regression. Summer vacation was just one week away, and I was hoping that my second visit to Jeroen would uncover information that would be helpful for our upcoming trip to New York in mid-July when we planned to visit significant landmarks from Lou Gehrig's life. This is something Dr. Tucker had suggested we do sooner than later because in August Christian would be turning six—the age when children's past-life memories generally disappear for good. In between visiting Lou Gehrig's old homes and taking Charlotte and Christian to a game at Yankee Stadium, I also planned to visit the National Baseball Hall of Fame Library in Cooperstown to continue my research.

I arrived at Jeroen's home at 10 A.M., knowing that our session would probably take a minimum of three hours. This time I was filled with hopeful exuberance, rather than fear, when I knocked on the door. During our pre-session chat, Jeroen warned me that the odds of going back to the same lifetime were slim. In his experience as a past-life regression therapist, none of his clients had ever repeated the same lifetime in subsequent regressions. He said, "Try to go in without any expectations." After hearing Jeroen's advice, I let go of the idea of visiting the life of Christina Gehrig for a second time and decided it might be fun to embark on a new adventure.

I took my place on the massage table, and within what felt like seconds, the visual imagery slowly came into focus. Jeroen asked me tell him how I was feeling and what my shoes looked like.

"I feel happy . . . and young."

When I looked down at my feet, I saw shiny, closed-toe shoes and a long dress with an apron in front and a long tie in the back.

"Who helps you with the tie?" he asked.

"My mom."

The setting I described was a green meadow with wild-flowers, and a lake to my right. I told him it was a party with my family to celebrate summer. I was four years old. I told him I could smell meat cooking and see boys playing horseshoes. Jeroen's continued probing revealed that I had blue eyes and long, blonde hair, which my mom some-times put up in a half ponytail.

"What is your favorite food you will be eating today?"

"*Kuchen*. White cake with strawberries and whipped cream."

From visiting my husband's family in Germany, I knew that *Kuchen* was the German word for cake, but it surprised me to hear the word cross my lips because I had never actually said it before. Through his questioning, Jeroen led me to my home. I immediately saw and described a farmhouse in the woods with a corrugated metal roof; I was sitting at the kitchen table. I told Jeroen I was eating porridge and cake with my mother and father. When Jeroen asked me about my father, I said, "He is a farmer kind of guy . . . cuts wood and stuff."

Jeroen prompted me to move on to the next important scene in the life of this young girl.

"One, two, three . . . what's happening now?"

I described myself as a pudgy 17-year-old who was a good student and living with my grandma.

With deep sadness in my voice, I told Jeroen, "My dad lives away somewhere. My mom died."

"Do you love anything or anyone in your life right now?"

"I want to move from this house. Go live somewhere else . . . It's hard to leave my grandma."

"What does your grandma call you?"

"Stina—for Christina—like a nickname. We take care of each other because my grandpa died too, so she is lonely."

The words came out of my mouth in such a rush that each time I said something, it felt as if I was listening to somebody else speaking.

I described dressing up to go to an outdoor market in the center of town where people sell food. I said I could see "firelights—like little candles in a row." Then I felt my face blush when I told Jeroen about a guy I liked—an older, adventurous businessman who wanted to move to

America too. Jeroen asked where I was living, and I said, "Feels like Europe, like Northern Germany." I told Jeroen I had some friends I described as, "Older kids who had moved to America . . . They send letters. There's opportunities there." A feeling of hope and optimism swept over me as I said these words.

Jeroen prompted me to move away from this scene and on to the next. He then asked what I was looking at or feeling. I giggled and said, "I think I'm pregnant." I described feeling happy but scared because I wasn't yet married to the baby's father—my boyfriend, Henry.

"Is that okay with your families? For you not to be married but have a baby on the way?"

I responded coyly, "They don't really know yet. We just got to America too."

I said we were staying with a family who didn't know about my pregnancy either, and I told him I was "cooking and cleaning to help pay for our room." When Jeroen asked what we brought with us to America, I said, "We brought a trunk filled with personal things; clothes, jewelry, and some pictures." I could perfectly see the full-color details of the items I was describing.

This is when he asked about our journey to America. I felt as if I was actually on the boat as I described sleeping on the top deck on a burlap blanket and seeing black steam coming out of the ship. I said we weren't able to take a shower on the 14-day trip, and we brought our own food to save money. I laughed when adding, "We brought some alcohol too!" He asked if it was a direct trip from Germany or if we had traveled to a different country, and I replied, "Iceland—North, I think." I described feeling relieved to get off of the boat in New York and told him I had to "sign in."

"What did the signing-in entail?"

"They wanted your name and your birthday and where you're from . . . We didn't have a lot of money with us. We just decided to stay in New York."

I felt happy as I described finding some people on the boat who spoke German too. I was particularly fond of my new friend Meredith Krueger, who'd made the trip with her brother. Jeroen asked what type of work Henry does. Without hesitation I said, "He works with his hands. Kind of like metal and tools. He might make horseshoes too." Jeroen asked what I like about New York, to which I replied, "I like the people. I like that everything's new. They are much happier here . . . I'm happy here." I felt very content and proud as I spoke about my new life in America.

"So, let's move forward to the day when your baby is born. Tell me what happens," Jeroen said.

"We didn't have a lot of money to pay a doctor, so we had to have friends help us at our house." When he asked how I felt about it, I surprised myself when the following words came out of my mouth, "Kind of sad, I think."

"Why are you feeling sad?"

My voice quivered as I replied, "It wasn't a good birth . . . the cord was wrapped around the neck of the baby."

I expressed my concern that the baby wasn't eating and said, "I think it was too traumatic, the birth. If we went to the doctor, I think he would have been okay."

I said my friends who'd helped with the birth "had done it before, but didn't really know what to do."

"It must have been hard for you," Jeroen empathized.

We were both shocked when I said, "Yeah, it's a sad feeling to bury a baby." In that moment, I experienced a deep sense of despair, as if I had lost a baby of my own.

"What was wrong with the baby?"

"He had a fever, but I still think it was the birth. It was just too hard on him."

I told him that by the time the doctor came to us it was too late, and I reported that the baby had died 12 days after the birth. My heart was heavy when I said, "I just wish we had made a better decision, had some help . . . I think Meredith Krueger helped me."

I felt the sadness lift when Jeroen instructed me to go to the next important scene for me to look at and experience. After the countdown he said, "What's happening now?" This time I was a mother and I happily described cleaning my two babies. I said the two-year-old boy would get jealous when I would breastfeed the one-year-old girl.

"But he's too big," I told Jeroen.

He asked me what the boy does when he gets jealous, and we both chuckled when I replied, "He tries to sit on my lap." I seemed confident that the boy's name was Lou, but when he asked me if I had a nickname for the little girl, I said, "I think her name is Sophie, but I don't know what I call her." I described her as petite with blue eyes and skin that was paler than Lou's. I added, "He loves her too." When he asked if she was a healthy baby, I replied, "Yeah. She's skinny. I need to fatten her up." I giggled.

The line of questioning then turned toward where we were living at the time. I expressed being happy to live in a cheap one-bedroom apartment we'd found outside of the city in a three- or four-story building made of bricks. He asked if my friend Meredith Krueger was still around, and I responded affectionately, "Yeah, she's a good friend . . . She loves my kids too." When I told Jeroen that she works a lot, as a secretary, he asked, "How do you feel about that?" I said, "I'm happy for her. I don't know if she can meet a man because she is so busy." Jeroen asked if I had married

Henry yet, and I replied with a big grin, "Yeah, we're married." When he asked about our ceremony, I chuckled while saying, "We just went to the courthouse. We didn't have a party or anything."

When Jeroen asked about my life as a mother, I felt a sense of pride and fulfillment when telling him about my day-to-day responsibilities of cooking, cleaning, and taking care of my two kids. When asked about my husband's line of work, I reported that he was now working at a shop where they make fences. Jeroen asked if we were doing okay with income, and I replied, "We're okay. I want to get pictures of the kids made, but it costs money." I was clearly worried about the money, but concluded, "I think I'm gonna do that."

Jeroen gave the instruction to move to the next important scene, and following the count of three, he asked his usual question, "What is happening now?"

"We had to bury our baby girl," I said calmly.

Sensing my sadness, Jeroen said, "Oh, no!"

I expressed being concerned about "poor Lou" and said, "He's just confused. Doesn't know where she went."

"How old is Lou now?"

"He is three."

"What happened to her?"

"She got a sickness, a fever, like a virus . . . a cough."

Jeroen asked if this was common, and I reflected with deep despair, "It happens. It happens. But I thought she would be okay. We tried everything."

"What did you try?"

"We tried like special foods, medicines, but we just couldn't save her."

I could see the little girl suffering when I said, "Her little body was so hot. It was an infection." I said she had died at sundown and mentioned having a priest there too. When Jeroen asked how Lou was handling her death, I said, "He just misses his baby. I hope he can have a baby one day."

"How is Henry dealing with this?" Jeroen asked.

"He is sad, but in the background . . . trying to work. I don't see him much."

When Jeroen asked about our relationship, I said, "He is quiet. Sometimes he yells. We're okay."

Lightening up the mood, Jeroen asked in an upbeat way, "Who's wearing the pants in the relationship?" My response was, "He's not a real strong person, not real communicative. I get to make more decisions . . . He doesn't have a lot of opinions."

Jeroen touched again on the loss of my baby and asked if I was okay with showing my feelings. I told him that I cry a lot, but not in front of Lou. I said with conviction, "I try to be strong for him."

At the end our session, while I was still in trance, Jeroen asked for permission to speak with the "subconscious of Cathy." He asked me about the purpose of this sequence of events.

"I think there is a picture of Lou and his sister somewhere," I told him, "Maybe I can find that picture when I go to New York."

When I left Jeroen's house, I couldn't shake the heaviness of the firsthand experience of losing two young children to untimely deaths. I vaguely recalled having read about Lou Gehrig having siblings who had died at young ages, but I never gave it much thought. I knew from the personal experience of my father losing his three-year-old sister to meningitis that death from childhood illnesses was common in the early 1900s. Lou Gehrig's deceased siblings never seemed important to me until this very sur-real experience where the pain of loss affected me deeply.

The first thing I did when I arrived home was look up Lou Gehrig's family tree on Ancestry.com. The site listed two siblings—Sophie, who was born one year after Lou and passed away at the age of one and a half, and a sister named Anna, who was born the year before Lou and lived only three months. Although it was quite a strange and morbid thing to do, I ordered the death and birth certifi-cates of Sophie and Anna Gehrig. When the documents arrived a few weeks later, it was Sophie Gehrig's death cer-tificate that caught my attention. It took my breath away when I read the cause of death was "Measles, Diphtheria, Broncho-Pneumonia." This explained the suffering I had described as well as the high fever and cough.

I read online that Lou was the only one of four Gehrig children to survive babyhood, but I was unable to find any record of the birth or death of a fourth child in the Gehrig family. I had a strong intuitive feeling that the mystery sibling must have been the little boy I'd described giving birth to prior to being married to Henry. While under hypnosis I had said we'd kept this pregnancy a secret from our parents and had never given the boy a name because he died 12 days after his birth. I wondered if Christina Gehrig's out-of-wedlock pregnancy, which I saw so clearly under hypnosis, was in fact real. If so, it must have been a secret she kept from the world—and from her own fam-ily—until the day she died. This would explain why the birth order of the fourth Gehrig child has always remained a mystery.

Many of the other details that had come up in my regression were difficult to verify, such as whether or not Christina really had a friend named Meredith Krueger.

However, I was able to find documentation confirming that Lou Gehrig's mother, Christina Facke, had come to America from Germany on a ship at the turn of the century when she was a teenager, exactly as I had reported. I also found out that the journey to America by boat often included a stop in Iceland. It was difficult to find information about Christina's childhood in Germany, but I was quite surprised to read that she did live with her grandmother. I wasn't able to determine if it was her maternal grandmother who she lived with, but I seemed very sure of this fact while under hypnosis. My Internet search also revealed that in Germany, "Stina" was once a common nickname for Christina, which I never knew before. I also discovered photographs from the late 1800s of German homes with corrugated metal roofs, similar to the one I saw when describing her childhood home to Jeroen.

My online search for a photo of Lou Gehrig with his baby sister was a complete bust. Unearthing this photo, if such a photo existed, became my new obsession. I sensed how important it had been to Christina Gehrig to get a photo of the two of them together, even though she couldn't afford it. I added searching for the photo to my list of things to do in New York. Surely if such a photo existed, it would be somewhere within the archives of the National Baseball Hall of Fame Library.

Shortly before our trip to New York, I finally mustered up the courage to tell Michael about my past-life regressions with Jeroen. As I predicted, he wasn't nearly as fascinated with my findings as I was and thought the whole thing was very odd. I didn't really blame him; he was right. The night before my big trip to New York with the kids, Michael and I watched the movie *The Pride of the Yankees*, a 1942 classic depicting Lou Gehrig's life story and starring

Gary Cooper. In the movie, Lou's mother was portrayed as a stern, overbearing German woman with no sense of humor. This was a stark contrast to the kindhearted—and sometimes funny—mother who had surfaced in my regressions.

I sat in disbelief when the movie portrayed Lou Gehrig prior to his retirement from the Yankees, receiving the news that he had very little time to live. This was in direct conflict with the very sure feeling I'd had that he would be okay while speaking in the first person as his mother.

"I'm positive that Lou Gehrig's mother had no idea that his illness was life threatening up until the moment of his death," I told Michael.

I'm sure he thought I had completely lost my mind when I pressed Rewind to watch the scene again, and emphatically argued, "There is *no way* that Lou knew he was going to die before he gave his 'Luckiest Man' speech!"

As crazy as it was, I couldn't let go of my intuitive feeling that the information that had surfaced through my past-life regression was correct and the movie was wrong.

CHAPTER EIGHTEEN

BASEBALL HEAVEN

"Progress always involves risks. You can't steal
second base and keep your foot on first."

FREDERICK B. WILCOX

A few days before our big trip to New York in July 2014,
a segment featuring Christian aired on FOX Sports as the
opening of the MLB All-Star Game Pregame Show.

The five-minute segment, which had taken nearly
five hours to film, featured Christian playing baseball
and talking about his dream of being an All-Star in the
Major Leagues. The footage of him pitching, hitting, sliding, catching, and sitting in the dugout was interspersed
with video highlights of actual MLB All-Star players from
over the years. At the conclusion of the segment, the
on-air commentator said, "That was five-year-old Christian Haupt. We may be seeing him someday at the All-
Star Game."

Christian's sixth birthday was one month away and,
just as Dr. Tucker had predicted, the memories he had
freely shared with us for the past three years seemed to be
evaporating like morning dew. I hoped that I hadn't waited
too long to make this trip to show him the significant

landmarks from Lou Gehrig's life. When he learned that our accommodations would be a small plywood cabin with no plumbing at a baseball camp near the National Baseball Hall of Fame in Cooperstown, New York, Michael decided to stay home and take care of our dogs. I think it was hearing about the 25-cent showers and potential creepy crawlers that cemented his decision to forego the trip.

In the weeks leading up to our trip, I used my Realtor skills to locate the names of the owners of the two homes that Lou Gehrig had lived in that were still standing. The first home I hoped to visit was located at 9 Meadow Lane in New Rochelle, New York. Lou had purchased this home for his parents in 1927 after signing his first big contract with the Yankees. The property profile revealed that the home was now owned by a man named Jimmy with a long Italian last name. The second was a home in Riverdale, where Lou lived with his wife, Eleanor, for the last two years of his life. I mailed letters to the respective owners, describing Christian's past-life memories and our intent to visit. I hoped the two current owners of the homes wouldn't slam the doors in our faces when we showed up at their doorsteps.

My last item of business in preparation for our trip was contacting the executives at the National Baseball Hall of Fame to ask for permission to access the Gehrig family's private documents and scrapbooks. I was on a mission to find a childhood photo of Lou Gehrig and his baby sister, and also on the hunt for any other clues that would validate or debunk Christian's past-life memories and my past-life regressions.

Our connecting flight from Chicago to the Albany International Airport was filled with people decked out in baseball attire, and Christian was excited when a nice man seated next to us offered to let him try on his Saint

Louis Cardinals World Series ring. We were arriving on the eve of the annual National Baseball Hall of Fame induction weekend, a time when the most celebrated names in baseball history convene in Cooperstown. Ironically 2014 was not only the 75th anniversary of the first induction ceremony at the National Baseball Hall of Fame but it was also the 75th anniversary of the day Lou Gehrig had heartbreakingly said good-bye to baseball with his iconic "Luckiest Man" speech at Yankee Stadium in front of 61,808 fans.

I found it ironic that even though Lou Gehrig was voted into the Hall of Fame while he was still alive, his formal induction ceremony did not take place until 2013. The 2014 Hall of Fame inductees would be Greg Maddux, Tom Glavine, Frank Thomas, and managers Joe Torre, Bobby Cox, and Tony La Russa. Our pal Tommy Lasorda had been making this trip to Cooperstown annually ever since being inducted into the Hall of Fame himself in 1997, but this year was extra special for him because his dear friend Joe Torre was going to be inducted.

After a one-night hotel stay in Albany, our last sleeping quarters with running water for the next week, Charlotte, Christian, and I embarked on our journey to America's baseball mecca. President Barack Obama's sojourn to Cooperstown two months prior to our arrival was the first time in history that a sitting president had ever visited the National Baseball Hall of Fame Museum. President Obama's sentiments while visiting Cooperstown were, "So I love baseball; America loves baseball. It continues to be our national pastime. And for any baseball fan out there, you've got to make a trip here."

Our Cooperstown trip was not inspired by the president, but by youth baseball coach Ali Cepeda. During the fall and winter months, Christian had played on a travel baseball team called the Cepeda Bulls, named after Hall of Fame baseball player (and Ali Cepeda's father) Orlando Cepeda. Ali Cepeda and his brother Malcolm, both of whom were also outstanding baseball players in their own rights, had been running a two-week overnight baseball camp at Cooperstown Beaver Valley Campground for the past few years to coincide with the National Baseball Hall of Fame induction weekend, where their father Orlando was honored every July.

Orlando Cepeda had come from Puerto Rico to play 16 seasons in the Majors, most prominently as a power-hitting first baseman with the Giants. Orlando's father, Pedro "Perucho" Cepeda, had earned the titles of "Babe Ruth of the Caribbean" and "The Bull," so when Orlando followed in his father's footsteps, he was affectionately referred to as "The Baby Bull." As of 2014 Orlando held the distinction of being the only Puerto Rican, besides Roberto Clemente, to ever be inducted into the National Baseball Hall of Fame.

I had booked our trip months in advance, after reading about the camp on the Cepeda Baseball website. It struck me as the perfect opportunity to take Christian to New York, as Dr. Tucker had suggested. The weekly rate for our tiny cabin in the woods was $350, a small price to pay at this time of year when a single night at a Cooperstown motel runs upwards of $350. On the day that we arrived, nearly 50,000 people had flocked to this provincial town to honor 58 of the 72 living National Baseball Hall of Fame members who would be present at the induction ceremony.

Google Maps took me right to the center of town, where we were greeted by a spectacular view of Otsego Lake, surrounded by lush green landscape as far as the eye could see. The Native Americans are said to have called the breathtaking lake "O-te-sa-ga," and James Fenimore Cooper called it "The Glimmerglass." Charlotte and Christian rolled down the windows of our rental car as we approached the marina, eager to explore. After skipping a few stones on the lake, our first stop would be lunch with Tommy Lasorda. We made our way onto Main Street, an experience reminiscent of stepping into a Norman Rockwell painting from the 1950s. We swam upstream through the sea of baseball fans in search of the only authentic Italian restaurant in town where we knew we would find Uncle Tommy.

Tommy Lasorda and Christian had developed a special bond that was palpable when they were together. At the restaurant, after Tommy and Christian exchanged a hug with mutual admiration, Tommy noticed Charlotte had a serious look on her face. He reached out and pulled her into the warmth of his big bear hug as he said, "You're such a beautiful girl, but we can't see it without a smile on your face." Following that warmhearted gesture, Charlotte managed to eke out a smile, and I remembered why I loved this man so much.

At nearly 87 years old, Tommy was still the hardest working man in baseball. The wedding ring on his arthritic left hand symbolized 60 years of marriage to his wife, Jo. Like Lou Gehrig, Tommy pitched and batted lefty, but was taught to write with his right hand, which was socially encouraged at the time. Today at lunch his right hand was working overtime as he signed his name over and over again on 8½ x 11-inch sheets of stickers embossed with 15 miniature baseballs per sheet. In between signing his name multiple times, he would take a sip of his red wine, a testament to his Italian heritage. When he finally took a break from signing to eat his pasta and salad, he said to his team of handlers seated at the table with us, "You wanna fix Little League baseball? Let the moms coach." He then told us that his love and respect for mothers comes from his love for his own mother, Carmella Lasorda, a warm and gracious Italian mother who'd always had something cooking on the stove and words of encouragement for her five boys.

Our next stop was Doubleday Field in the heart of Cooperstown, where famed baseball writer Roger Angell would be receiving the J. G. Taylor Spink Award for "meritorious contributions in baseball writing." At 93 years old, Roger Angell was a graceful master of prose for *The New Yorker* for five decades and counting. In a tribute to the great game of baseball, Angell said, "My gratitude always goes back to baseball itself, which turned out to be so familiar and so startling, so spacious and exacting. So easy-looking and so heartbreakingly difficult that it filled up my notebooks and the seasons in a rush. A pastime, indeed."

In his acceptance speech, Angell credited his mother, Katharine Sergeant Angell White, who was the first fiction editor at *The New Yorker*, and his stepfather, E. B. White, who authored *Charlotte's Web* and *The Elements of Style*, for introducing him to the literary world. Not quite understanding the significance of the award, my kids managed to patiently and quietly sit through the speeches. One of the highlights was getting to meet an amiable 96-year-old man by the name of Homer Osterhoudt, who had not missed a Hall of Fame induction ceremony since the first one he had attended in 1939.

After loading up on groceries and a few essential items for our baseball camp in the woods, we headed out of town and into the hills to find the campground that would be our home for the next five days. By the time we arrived, it was dark, raining, and very cold. I was starting to think Michael may have been wise in his choice to sit this one out. Wearing our newly purchased rain ponchos, we found our way to the communal restrooms, and then hunkered down in our sparsely appointed home away from home.

CHAPTER NINETEEN

THE PRIDE
OF THE YANKEES

"The important thing is not to stop questioning.
Curiosity has its own reason for existing."
ALBERT EINSTEIN

I peeked out the front door of our cabin shortly after sunrise the next morning and was overwhelmed by the beauty of the place that had felt daunting and mysterious the night before. About 50 yards from our doorstep was a baseball field right out of the movie *Field of Dreams*, framed by a baby-blue sky, white clouds, and rolling hills, thick with trees that we see in California only at higher elevations. After thoroughly enjoying our 25-cent showers, Charlotte, Christian, and I made our way to the cafeteria to greet our hosts. I walked up behind a man who I thought was my friend Ali Cepeda decked out in San Francisco Giants gear, but when he turned around, I was greeted by an unfamiliar, yet familiar face. It turned out to be Ali's brother Malcolm Cepeda.

After a quick introduction, Malcolm treated me to some family folklore. He shared a personal story of how his father, Orlando Cepeda, had been scheduled to fly to Nicaragua to deliver aid to earthquake victims on the same flight that took the life of the legendary Latin American baseball player Roberto Clemente on December 31, 1972. Malcolm told me how fate had intervened when his father decided not to take the flight because he didn't want to leave his one-month-old baby boy (Malcolm) at home. Thankfully Orlando chose to stay home with his family, and four years later, his son Ali was born. Following the tragic death of Roberto Clemente in 1972, Orlando went on to become an All-Star slugger who ranked among the top hitters of all time.

Ali and Malcolm have dedicated their adult lives to preserving their father's legacy through the family's non-profit youth baseball organization, Cepeda Baseball. The first time I ever met Ali, he said, "I believe baseball is the reason why I was put on this Earth." He told me that nothing pleases him more than the opportunity to share his knowledge and passion for the sport with kids who have an equal love of the game. Christian was elated to wake up to Wiffle ball games every morning, followed by seven hours of baseball camp. While he was having the time of his life playing baseball with the Cepedas and their staff of collegiate coaches, I spent each day scouring the archives of the Giamatti Research Center at the nearby National Baseball Hall of Fame with Charlotte at my side. She was happy to play games on her computer for hours on end while I looked through piles of legal documents, scrapbooks, and newspaper articles on Lou Gehrig, many of which had been donated to the museum by Lou Gehrig's mother and wife. Each day the very helpful manager of the Giamatti Research Center would bring down a large cart filled with boxes containing the documents I had requested prior to my trip. The nearly 100-year-old documents were normally kept in a climate-controlled storage area in the Hall of Fame archives, and many of them had to be handled with white gloves due to their fragility. I was guessing this was the first time they had been out of the vault in many years.

My first interesting discovery was information contained in private legal documents donated by Eleanor Gehrig that pointed to an ongoing feud between herself and Lou's parents, Henry and Christina Gehrig. Via their respective attorneys, Lou's wife and parents had argued about everything from where Lou Gehrig's final resting place should be to whether or not Lou's parents were the rightful beneficiaries of a life insurance policy he had purchased for them. In the file was a letter to Eleanor from her own attorney, outlining a plan to have the Gehrigs removed as beneficiaries. The letter read:

Mom Gehrig is a German subject and whatever money she may have on deposit may be frozen.

I subsequently found a legal document stating that Eleanor Gehrig was ultimately successful in having Henry and Christina Gehrig's rights to Lou's life insurance payout revoked by proving that the Gehrigs were still German citizens. I hadn't been a fan of Eleanor Gehrig before finding this information, but now, her treatment of Lou Gehrig's parents struck me as downright cruel.

Another letter I came across stated that the only money Eleanor ever gave the Gehrigs from their son's estate was $5.00 to purchase the death certificate for Lou's father upon his passing. I found it strange that the receipt for payment of the $5.00 for the death certificate had been donated to the National Baseball Hall of Fame by Eleanor Gehrig. The fact that Eleanor was so willing to air her dirty laundry by donating these documents led me to believe she must have been proud of her actions. I was saddened by my discoveries and was starting to dislike Lou Gehrig's wife more and more with each passing day. She wasn't just a "funny lady," as I had declared during my regression; she was heartless.

Of all the documents I came across during my fact-finding mission at the National Baseball Hall of Fame Library, the golden nugget was a typed letter from the mother of Lou Gehrig's wife, Eleanor, addressed to Christina Gehrig's attorney. Lou Gehrig's mother-in-law Nellie Twitchell wrote in the letter:

Then came Lou's illness. For a year he was doctored for gallbladder trouble. A prominent physician mistakenly diagnosed his case as such. He slipped in baseball. Eleanor started to show signs of extreme worry. And to make it short, ultimately Lou went to the Mayo Clinic.

Immediately Eleanor was notified that Lou had at most three years to live. Luckily, he was away when she was informed. For two weeks my daughter sat in a chair all night with a grief I have never before witnessed. And then a day before Lou's return, she made herself as presentable as possible, set her jaw, and made ready for the finest bit of courage known.

I lived with them both after this, and I can tell you that until Lou breathed his last (breath) he did not know he was going to die. Eleanor had all the doctors fixed, all their friends fixed—to bolster Lou's morale. And as day by day he became more paralyzed, the strain became greater on my daughter. She never faltered.

I could barely believe what I had read even though I had already known it in my heart to be true. Lou Gehrig and his parents were never told that his illness was life threatening!

I whipped out my phone at the table and called Michael right away to tell him what I had found. I'm sure I startled the other researchers in the close quarters of the National Baseball Hall of Fame Library when I said:

"Michael! The movie *Pride of the Yankees* was wrong, and my regression was right! Lou and his parents were never told that he was going to die."

Lowering my voice, I methodically explained the contents of the letter to Michael. My suspicion was confirmed: Lou Gehrig had no clue that his death was imminent when he delivered his "Luckiest Man" retirement speech at Yankee Stadium.

The letter also gave details about a horrible fight between Eleanor and Christina Gehrig that had estranged Lou from his parents for the last three months of his life. Eleanor's mother wrote that the fight began when the two ladies were in the kitchen while Lou was asleep in the other room. According to Lou's mother-in-law, Eleanor exploded after Christina said to her, "Dry beans are better for vitamins. If Louie had stayed with me, this never would have happened!" Of Eleanor's reaction, her mother wrote:

Eleanor became incensed, and in a gush told Mom of every unhappiness Mom had caused. In a torrent of words she said everything that had been pent up so long. In closing Eleanor said, "You and your cooking, look at Pop, - he is epileptic, - look at yourself, - you have blood pressure and heart trouble, and that boy upstairs is sick, - now look at me – look at Nel – look at Bud, - we are so healthy. Maybe some day when

*the cause of this disease is known it might be you who
will blush.*

I couldn't help but think how sad Lou's mother must
have been when Lou died less than three months after this
argument. *Could this be the "yelling" that Christian had spoken of when we talked about Lou Gehrig's wife that one night
before bed?* I had a strong feeling that Lou's parents were
not able to say proper good-byes to their son during the
months, weeks, and days leading up to his passing, due to
the rift between Christina and Eleanor.

I waited until my last day at the National Baseball Hall
of Fame Giamatti Research Center to make a trip to the
photo archives to retrieve the photos of Lou Gehrig. In
retrospect I think my hesitation to look at the photos was
due to my fear that I might not be able to find the photo
of Lou Gehrig and his baby sister from my regression that
I so desperately wanted to locate.

A friendly employee named John, who was responsible
for maintaining the photo archives, treated Charlotte and
me to a tour of the frigid 55-degree vault where all of the
photos that had been donated to the museum over the
past 75 years were stored. I was awestruck to see aisle after
aisle of countless photos hanging in file folders from floor
to ceiling. The sleeveless tops and shorts Charlotte and I
were wearing did not adequately prepare us for the experience of walking into what felt like a refrigerator in the
middle of summer.

After gathering all the Lou Gehrig folders from the *G*
section, we returned to the research library. I donned my
white gloves and attacked the 12 file folders like a wild
animal on a hunt for prey. After sorting through photos
for an hour, I came to the last file in the huge stack labeled

Gehrig Family. Photo one, photo two, photo three. Then, at the bottom of the pile of photos . . . there it was.

My gloved fingers trembled as I picked it up: a photo of young Lou Gehrig and his baby sister riding in a horse-drawn carriage together. I could have cried. Lou was seated in the front seat of the carriage holding on to the reigns of the horse with a big smile on his face. Beside him was an elderly woman with her arm around Lou, and seated on the woman's lap was a baby wearing a white bonnet. *It had to be Sophie!*

My heart raced with joy as I held the black-and-white photo, which had yellowed over the years, in my hands. I was relieved to know that Christina Gehrig was able to fulfill her dream of having a photo taken of her children together prior to her daughter Sophie's death. Of all the scenes I experienced during my past-life regressions, Christina's short-lived time as a mother of two children appeared to be the happiest time of her life. Seeing the photo made me think about the sibling bond between Charlotte and Christian. My heart ached for Christina Gehrig.

On the last day of baseball camp, Charlotte and I got in on the action during the parents-versus-kids scrimmage, where the kids who had participated in the camp pitched to their respective family members. Christian loved trying to strike us out, although he was unsuccessful in the attempt. On our way out of town, we made one last stop at the National Baseball Hall of Fame Museum, where Christian and Charlotte reveled in taking photos of all the exhibits. We then drove four hours to the Bronx to see one of Derek Jeter's final games as a Yankee. Christian became Derek Jeter's number one fan after I told him that Derek was the first Yankee in history to break Lou Gehrig's all-time hitting record.

I was a little nervous about knocking on the doors of Lou Gehrig's old homes, so I saved that task for our last full day in New York. As we drove up to the home at 9 Meadow Lane in New Rochelle, I had a feeling of déjà vu. The white house sat on top of a hill and looked exactly like the home I had seen and described while under hypnosis. Christian took pictures of the house and Charlotte took pictures of Christian taking pictures of the house as we made our way up the steep, grassy front yard.

We followed Christian's lead as he ran up the steps to the enclosed porch and knocked on the front door. We were greeted by the friendly and charismatic owner of the home, Jimmy, and with a classic New York accent he introduced us to his lovely girlfriend, Marisol. Without acknowledging my letter directly, he implied that he was aware of our plan to visit and kindly invited us inside to take a tour of the home. I'm guessing the floor plan had remained the same ever since Lou Gehrig purchased the home in 1927, because the home appeared to be untouched by the modern world, with the exception of a few new appliances. While Marisol stayed busy in the kitchen, her nine-year-old nephew and their two cats, Tiger and Sofia, followed us from room to room in the four-story home.

Jimmy's tour even included a peek into the basement. When I saw the basement bathroom, which was still equipped with the original bathtub and chain-pull toilet from when the home was built in 1905, I found myself daydreaming about days gone by. He told us the basement bathroom was most likely built back in the day so that the coal workers wouldn't need to come into the main house to wash off when delivering coal. Up in the attic, Jimmy pointed out an old, cedar closet and a light fixture that was originally plumbed for gas. Jimmy was amused when

I shared the story of how Christian had told us about his childhood home having "fire in the lights" when he was a kid before. I explained that this was my first time ever seeing a gas-fueled light fixture because most of the homes in our Southern California community were built after 1960.

As we stood on the enclosed porch of the big, white house at 9 Meadow Lane where Lou Gehrig lived with his parents from 1927 to 1933, Christian looked lost in thought for a moment.

"This is where Babe Ruth used to smoke," he said.

I knew from my research that Babe Ruth was a frequent visitor to the home on Meadow Lane and even lived with the Gehrig family for a year after the death of his first wife. I also knew that Babe was well known for his gregarious drinking and smoking, but these were not things Christian was ever made aware of.

As we departed Jimmy told us a story about an elderly man who had told him he used to deliver newspapers to the Gehrig family at that address as a child. Jimmy said the man always hoped that Lou's mother would be the one to answer the door when he arrived because she was a good tipper, unlike Lou who never gave him a tip and was known for being a spendthrift. I laughed when telling Jimmy that my son was the only child I've ever known who returned everything he ever bought with his own money because of regrets about spending. "Perhaps old habits die hard," Jimmy joked, "You know, this house was one of the only big purchases Lou Gehrig ever made. It's the only home he ever owned."

Before going to the airport to head home to Los Angeles, we made a stop in Valhalla, New York where the ashes of Lou Gehrig and his parents are buried. Christian's mood was serious when he placed a flower on Lou's tombstone.

Even Charlotte, who sometimes teased him about being Lou Gehrig, respected the significance of the moment by reaching out to hold her brother's hand as she read the names inscribed on the tombstones to him. I found it ironic that the final resting place of Christina and Henry Gehrig was just a few feet away from that of Lou's wife Eleanor Gehrig, given their tumultuous relationships. It was a very special and unforgettable moment for all three of us when Christian said his final good-byes to the man who had consumed his existence for the past three years.

Soon after we got home, one of Christian's baseball buddies challenged him to participate in the ALS Ice Bucket challenge that was sweeping the nation in July and August of 2014. Charlotte was delighted by the opportunity to dump a big bucket of icy water on her little brother's head, and Christian, who was well aware by now that ALS had taken Lou Gehrig's life, loved every last drop.

Christian's stories about his life as Lou Gehrig dwindled drastically after our visit to the cemetery that day. Our trip to New York, originally planned as an expedition to reignite Christian's past-life memories, turned out to provide the closure I had been hoping for since Dr. Tucker's visit four months earlier—closure for Christian and for our entire family.

CHAPTER TWENTY

FAMILY HEIRLOOMS

"For, you see, so many out-of-the-way things had
happened lately, that Alice had begun to think that
very few things indeed were really impossible."

LEWIS CARROLL, *ALICE'S ADVENTURES IN WONDERLAND*

In the fall of 2014, Christian's past-life recollections appeared to be taking a backseat to regular six-year-old activities, such as playing AYSO soccer and riding his bike with the neighborhood kids. Much to my delight, he was suddenly no longer interested in talking about his life as Lou Gehrig before bedtime. Instead he begged me to read him books like *Froggy Plays T-Ball* and *Casey at the Bat.* I think the nail in the coffin for his past-life memories was when the neighborhood kids made fun of him for saying that he was Lou Gehrig. When I heard Christian come through the front door sobbing, I rushed out of my home office to see if he was injured. I found him collapsed on the floor with his head in his hands and his back up against the closed door. When I asked him what had happened, he gasped for breath and said through his tears, "Nobody believes I was Lou Gehrig."

My heart sank when I realized that Christian had shared his very intimate secret with his playmates, some of whom were five or six years older than him. I never wanted him to be ashamed of talking about his past-life memories, however I probably would have warned him that other people might not understand—if I had ever imagined him making a public declaration that he *was* Lou Gehrig. As heartbreaking as it was to see my son completely disillusioned, this incident served its purpose by propelling Christian out of the past and into the present. He was finally ready to be Christian Haupt.

I thought I was also done exploring my personal connection to Christina Gehrig that had surfaced through my past-life regressions until I went to see Jeroen for a third time and inadvertently slipped back down into the rabbit hole. Jeroen had offered me a complimentary past-life regression in return for a workshop I had treated him to and I decided to take him up on his generous offer in November 2014.

Without any prompting from Jeroen, which is his standard practice, I once again ended up right back in the life of Christina Gehrig. The scene did not come into focus immediately, but as he questioned me about my surroundings, the images began to materialize. The first thing I saw was a small dog that I described as "a boy dog." I said he was sitting beside me on a "stiff couch" with a "low back," and under my feet was what I described as "a woven rug." When Jeroen asked me to describe what I looked like, I said I was female with white skin and blue eyes, a "bigger" body type, and a round face with glasses. I could feel aching pain in my hands telling him: "I am knitting or something . . . My hands are a little tired and sore. A little old, I think. They are arthritic, I think."

"What are you wearing?" Jeroen asked.

With my eyes closed, I glanced down at my body. "A big dress, almost like a robe . . . house shoes, not really slippers, but enclosed shoes." Each time Jeroen directed my attention to something new in my environment, the details came to life in my mind. He asked if I was wearing a hat, and I replied, "No, but I have my hair up, though, up on the back of my head, like a bun. My hair is gray."

When Jeroen asked what I was feeling, I said with a heavy heart, "A little sadness."

He quickly changed the topic to a lighter subject.

"What is the weather like?"

"It is kind of cool outside. There is a window to my left. It's chilly. Everything looks a bit frozen."

Jeroen followed up by asking, "Is the place heated?" I said there was a stove heater in the corner of the room, a wooden coffee table with newspapers on it, and a tall lamp near the couch.

When Jeroen asked me what the walls looked like, I replied, "Like plaster walls, and wood floor, and kind of a raised foundation. Not on the ground, up a little higher."

I recall looking out of the window to my left and seeing a rather large front yard with a gravel driveway to the right of the house with parked cars. I told Jeroen there were other people living in the house.

"Are they in the same room too?"

I described a lady cooking in the kitchen and smiled when telling Jeroen, "She's my friend." Jeroen then asked what it smelled like, and I said, "Some bread. I think their family is gonna come home for lunch." I can still remember the smell of the bread baking in the oven as if

I had really been there. Jeroen asked if I was living with the family.

"Yeah, with the family."

Jeroen gently inquired, "What about you, do you have a family?"

"No, I have my dog," I said with a laugh.

It was clear to me in that moment that this was the same good-humored woman Jeroen and I had met in my earlier past-life regressions.

"How do you spend the majority of your time?" Jeroen asked.

"I just keep busy reading, knitting, crossword puzzles sometimes."

When he asked if I do any activities outside of the house, I told him that I drive sometimes. I described my car as "grayish-black, not real shiny . . . with a big tail end . . . a Ford or Chrysler or something like that." In response to his question about what the house looked like, I replied, "It's got siding on the outside, like slats of wood on the outside, white." He asked how many floors the house had, and at first I said, "One," but immediately changed my mind and said, "No, wait. There are stairs, but I don't go up there. The kids might be upstairs. The stairs are wood too."

Then Jeroen asked, "How old are the kids?"

I felt a warm smile come to my face as I replied, "A couple of boys, like eleven and twelve, and a little girl. Maybe ten- and twelve-year-old boys. They are sweet. I like being around family . . . They were nice to take me in. I kind of ran out of money. I have a little bit left, not really enough for a house. I used to have a house here." I told Jeroen the family I lived with was much younger than me, but we had in common that they also came over from Germany and liked baseball too.

This is when our conversation turned to Christina Gehrig's passion for baseball. Jeroen inquired, "You say baseball?"

I replied, "I think the little boys play Little League. I go watch the games nearby." My voice became almost jovial when saying, "I like to bring treats for the boys, cookies." When Jeroen asked what kind of cookies, I said proudly, "I make 'em. Chocolate chip, oatmeal."

Jeroen said, "I bet they like that."

I nodded in agreement and giggled while saying, "Yeah. They kind of expect them now. I can't show up empty-handed. They sometimes run around my car when I'm coming there."

My mood quickly became somber when Jeroen again asked me, in a serious tone, if I had any family of my own. A deep feeling of despair enveloped me as I explained that both my son and my husband had passed away.

"How do you deal with your loss?"

"People still love him and they always tell me every day. They think of him, my son. My husband kind of gave up after my son died."

In response to Jeroen's question as to whether I had any other kids, I said, "He had a wife, but she's just different." My logical mind was telling me that Christina Gehrig couldn't stand the lady, even though the words coming out of my mouth were fairly kind.

When Jeroen asked if I had any brothers or sisters, I told him that my father had remarried and had two kids after my mom died, but that they lived in Germany.

"You've had a lot of loss," Jeroen said.

The somber mood lifted when I perked up and jokingly said, "Yeah. I got my animals to keep me company."

"More than the dog?"

"I've had a couple of birds. I have one now."

I told him I kept the bird in a big, iron cage near the couch and said, "I cover it at night when it sleeps. That bird I've had a long time." I described sticking my hand into the cage to take it out sometimes.

Just as our conversation was getting lighter, Jeroen asked where my husband and son were buried. I said it was a big drive to visit their graves because they were buried in New York, near where we used to live. This is when my logical mind started silently questioning if I was just reciting things I already knew; I had just visited Lou Gehrig's graveside in New York four months earlier.

"Do you go by yourself when you go?"

"Yeah, I do. I've done that by myself before—bring flowers. There's always a lot of people there at the grave, at my son's grave. They leave little things there for him."

My cynical mind was nowhere to be found when a peaceful feeling took over my body and I said, "I still feel connected to him. I kind of have a feeling he watches me." Then Jeroen asked if I keep any of my son's stuff anywhere. I said, "I have like a wooden chest that I keep some things in, a few things . . . old uniforms, jewelry."

When Jeroen asked if my son had left a lot of money behind, I replied, "Yeah, but the wife took it. She likes Hollywood. She lives the rich lifestyle."

"Where is she?"

"She might be in Hollywood," I replied. My breathy laugh let Jeroen know I was joking. I then answered his question in a more serious manner by saying, "I don't know, maybe New York City. I'm not a big fan of hers." Jeroen asked how I support myself, and I said, "I get some money from the government, a little bit. I sold everything

I had. I don't have much left. I sold my house. That money didn't last too long."

Shifting the conversation again, Jeroen asked me about the family I live with. I said affectionately of the woman in the kitchen, "I'm kind of like a mother to her though because she is younger. She kind of looks out for me." Jeroen asked me to describe what she looks like, and I replied, "She's pretty. Kind of heavier, like I am. She is cooking a lot, wearing kind of long dresses like I wear." When he asked me about her hair, I said, "Kind of brown hair with curls. Wears it kind of off her face, but not up—kind of like a headband-type thing." I added, "She doesn't work outside of the house. Her husband works."

When he asked me the ages of the kids a second time, I responded, "The boys are like ten and eleven. The girl is maybe like seven . . . She has short, dark hair." I felt proud and sounded very happy when saying, "My English is pretty good now too. The crossword puzzles help, and I still get *The New York Times*."

"What parts do you like reading?"

"The sports, I still keep an eye on. And things on the community—like entertainment and stuff." I said my son "Louie" had taught me a lot.

"Were you with your son when he died?"

"I remember being in the room, but I can't remember if it was right when he died. I can remember seeing him kind of unconscious." He asked if I was able to see him before he went, and I answered, "A little bit. She barely let us see him. She wanted to control it." I fondly reminisced, "He was a good son. He was a good person." Jeroen asked if Lou's wife got in between us and I said, "Yeah. She just took charge. He kind of just fell right into it. He let her be the boss." I expressed being sad that it had changed our relationship and added, "She was a little jealous of me, so she kind of wanted to cut him off."

Jeroen asked if I had any memorabilia to remember my son by, and I perked up when saying, "Very little. Just that one uniform, and then that coin from Japan. And then some jewelry that he bought me, like a bracelet and a necklace."

"A necklace?" Jeroen inquired.

"A pendant with jade in it. I don't have much family so I don't know where it'll—what to do with it. I don't know who to give it to."

"Are you thinking about that?"

"Yeah, when I die."

He followed up by asking, "What are you deciding about who to give it to?"

Without hesitation, I replied, "I could give it to the little girl, I guess. Probably have to give it to her mother to hold on to."

Jeroen instructed me to leave the scene and to go to the next important day. I described myself as a mother of two young kids and told him we were all dressed up.

"Is it a special day?"

"Yeah. It's like a Sunday, a church day . . . I feel like a baptism day."

I told him the baby girl was wearing a white dress and we were walking on a dusty dirt road. We were walking to church.

"Is it big or small?"

"It's small. Just like a one room church, white, not fancy, a Lutheran church, not a lot of people—there's a lot of German people there. We don't go all the time, but we're going today for the baby. She's gonna be baptized."

Jeroen asked if anybody else was with us and I said, "Yeah. Henry and his mom . . . or sister, I think. Visiting maybe, just for the baptism." I told Jeroen the boy's name was Lou.

"Has he been baptized yet?"

"Yeah. We did it when he was a baby. Now he's two. He's got knickers on. He is big though. He is a big kid. He looks like he is about four. He's got big hands, big feet, a big head. Not chubby, just big. He's sweet with the baby. He likes to hold her on his lap."

"So how did you get to church?"

"I think we walked, but I think the kids rode in the carriage for a little bit with the horses. That was fun they got to do that."

"You didn't do that?"

"No, it costs money."

"And you've got to be careful with money?"

"Yeah."

In the final scene of this past-life regression session, I described my old, tired body lying in a hospital bed, exactly as I had seen in my first regression with Jeroen.

"What do you look like lying in the bed?"

"Just a little old, tired, a little thinner than I was."

Showing a wry sense of humor, I added with a laugh, "Not thin though."

Curious about the jewelry I had mentioned earlier in the regression, Jeroen asked, "What about the jewelry?"

"I think I gave that to them."

"What kind of jewelry was it?"

I could see the items perfectly in my mind while describing them to Jeroen. "A gold necklace with a jade pendant, and a bracelet, like a charm bracelet. A watch."

He asked where I had gotten the jewelry, and I gushingly said, "From Lou. He always brought me things."

Detecting the love in my voice, Jeroen said, "He was a sweet kid, huh?"

I sighed, "Yeah."

Jeroen concluded the session by asking me to think about the lesson of this lifetime. I reflected for a moment and said, "Learning to accept loss."

"How did you do with that?"

"I think I did pretty well. I kind of kept my eye on the ball," I said with a laugh, showing Mom Gehrig's playful sense of humor once again. "I kind of kept charging along. I didn't get bitter."

"You didn't get bitter?"

"No. I think always being around kids always helped me."

Jeroen said, "They'll probably miss you too?"

I nodded and added, "Yeah. I might have been a little burden, but we had fun."

Jeroen gently eased me out of the trance and it was comforting to see his smiling face when I opened my eyes. I felt as if our journey into the life of Christina Gehrig was complete. We hugged good-bye and I made it back home with enough time to stop at our house before picking up Charlotte and Christian from school. I rushed to my home office and pulled out the photo of Lou and Sophie Gehrig I had discovered at the National Baseball Hall of Fame. A wave of emotion swept over me as I stared at the photograph through new eyes. They were all dressed in white, what looked to be their Sunday's finest. I now knew the story behind the photograph and had an even deeper understanding of Christina Gehrig's love for her children.

The difference between this past-life regression and my prior regressions was that the information coming through was not verifiable through research, but only by the very remote possibility of finding this family I had seen so clearly while under hypnosis—if they indeed existed and were still alive. Since Lou Gehrig's mother died in 1954, exactly 60 years earlier, the children I described would now be in their 70s, which would mean the parents would most likely be in their 90s. Finding the three children I had seen so clearly while under hypnosis became my new obsession. Not only did I not know if such a family existed in real life, but I also had no clue about the surname of the family because Jeroen hadn't asked me that during our session.

After returning home from picking up the kids, I began my investigation. I sifted through the documents I had copied at the National Baseball Hall of Fame Library and found a letter dated two weeks after Christina Gehrig's death in 1954. The letter was written by an employee of the National Baseball Hall of Fame to a man named Mr. George Steigler, who appeared to be a friend of Mrs. Gehrig:

> *Dear Mr. Steigler:*
> *The photographs, and negatives thereof, which you requested are being sent to you today.*
> *We hope you, your family and your friends will enjoy them.*

If the National Baseball Hall of Fame was going out of their way to send Christina Gehrig's photographs to the Steigler family, I assumed they must have been important people in her life. My online search revealed an obituary for George K. Steigler's wife, Laurel Steigler, who had passed away just five months earlier at the age of 95. The obituary listed her survivors as a daughter named Jill, who was a Realtor in Connecticut, and a son named Kenneth, who was a pastor in North Carolina. *Could this be the 7-year-old little girl and 10-year-old little boy I had seen in my regression?* I was still stumped about my description of three children in the home because only two children were listed in the obituary.

Being a Realtor myself, and considering my horrible experience of talking about Christian's past-life memories with our pastor, I decided to call Jill. When she answered on the first ring, I explained to her that I was doing research on Lou Gehrig and his family. Jill confirmed right away that Lou Gehrig's mother did indeed live with her family when she was a child. Unfortunately, she didn't recall any specific memories about Christina Gehrig, but she did remember her being a sweet and stoic woman.

As Jill spoke, I pictured her as the little girl with short, brown hair from my regression. She said her brother, Ken, who was three years older than her, might remember more details about the time when Mom Gehrig lived with them. I nearly choked when Jill said her brother was three years older than her because that fit perfectly with the ages of the 7-year-old girl and 10-year-old boy I had seen and described to Jeroen. As our conversation came to a close, I resisted the urge to ask her if she had inherited a charm bracelet and jade necklace from Japan that had belonged to Christina Gehrig out of fear that I would scare her away forever. That question was far too personal for a first phone call, but I knew the time would come when I would get up the courage to ask about Lou Gehrig's mother's most cherished possessions.

CHAPTER TWENTY-ONE

HEAVEN SENT

"Science cannot solve the ultimate mystery of nature.
And that is because, in the last analysis, we ourselves
are a part of the mystery that we are trying to solve."

MAX PLANCK

Two months passed before I garnered the courage to
track down Reverend Kenneth Steigler. As curious as I
was to find out if he had any memory of Christina Gehrig living with his family in the early 1950s, my fears
about how he might react to our story kept me immobi-
lized. Rather than asking Reverend Kenneth's sister for his
contact information, I decided to track him down via the
Internet. My search for *Reverend Kenneth Steigler* led me to
an article in *Christianity Today* entitled "Good News for
Witches," chronicling his outreach to witches as the head
pastor of the Wesley United Methodist Church in Salem,
Massachusetts.

According to the article, Reverend Kenneth and his
congregation of 265 members went out of their way to welcome witches with open arms, particularly in the month
of October—a time of year when the city is flooded with
tourists, partygoers, dabblers in witchcraft, and committed

witches who regard Halloween as their sacred day. Reverend Steigler was quoted as saying, "If 10 people go away from Salem thinking, 'There is a church that welcomed me, that loved me, even with all my amulets and all my stuff,' then all of it is worth our while." I also located a bio for Reverend Kenneth that said he had worked with Dr. Martin Luther King Jr. in his early 20s while he was a seminary student, and had recently led numerous tours to the Hebrew University of Jerusalem in Israel, where he was currently working on a doctoral studies degree in Biblical Theology. This sounded like a man who had seen just about everything, and it gave me hope that he wouldn't be too shocked by our story.

The next item on my supersleuth agenda was checking out the Salem Wesley United Methodist Church website. I struck gold when I found a trailer for Reverend Kenneth's short film, *Praying for Salem,* about his outreach to witches. My intuitive feeling after seeing him speak in the video was that this man of the cloth was a very loving person with a sincere commitment to serve others. After my call to the church was greeted by an answering machine, I decided to reach out to a man by the name of Dimitris, who was listed as contact person for the *Praying for Salem* video. When I told Dimitris the purpose of my call was to locate a phone number for Reverend Kenneth, he jubilantly exclaimed, "Pastor Ken is the most wonderful man on the planet, and I wouldn't be alive to answer this phone today without him!"

Dimitris went on to explain how Pastor Ken's comforting words gave him the will to live at a difficult time in his life, 12 years earlier, when he had lost his son and contemplated suicide. According to Dimitris, Ken was still a pastor emeritus for the church in Salem where he had been the head pastor for 16 years. Dimitris told me that Pastor Ken and his wife, Marilyn, now lived in North Carolina. He described his dear friend as a man who was never without a smile on his face, a man who was loved and revered by his congregation. He said the pastor was notorious for making himself available by cell phone to anybody who needed him, at any time of the day or night. Dimitris willingly provided me with Pastor Ken's cell phone number and his last words before ending our call were, "I hope when I meet God in Heaven, he looks a lot like Pastor Ken."

Just as Dimitris had predicted, Reverend Ken answered my call on the first ring. Not wanting to scare him off right away, I eased into the conversation by telling him I was researching the life of Christina Gehrig for a book I was writing. As much as I wanted to share the true purpose of my call, telling a pastor that your son thinks he was Lou Gehrig in a previous lifetime and you're wondering if his family inherited jewelry from Lou Gehrig's mother isn't something that flows easily off of the tongue. It was soon obvious that talking about "Mom Gehrig," as Ken called her, was one of his favorite pastimes. I was in awe of the wonderful memories he enthusiastically shared with me of this woman who he said was, "like a grandmother" to him. It almost felt as if he was describing scenes directly from my past-life regressions as he rattled off details that were shockingly consistent with what I had seen and described while in trance.

Pastor Ken gleefully reminisced about being a passenger in Mom Gehrig's big, black car—which he said she drove like a tank—when she took him to Yankees games as a young boy. He guessed the car was nearly 20 years old at the time. Ken fondly recalled entering the private back entrance to the stadium and being in awe when the fans who spotted her yelled, "Here comes Mom Gehrig!" With the hidden agenda of exploring the historical accuracy of the things I had seen and said under hypnosis, I asked Pastor Ken if he had ever played Little League as a kid. He laughed and said, "I did! Even though I was far from the best player on the team, Mom Gehrig was always there in the stands rooting for me."

A couple of seconds later, he had me in stitches as he shared stories about Mom Gehrig's pet bird, Polly. Ken said that before Mom Gehrig moved in with his family, she had her own home not too far away, and he would ride his bike there weekly to mow her lawn. One day he knocked on the door to let her know he was there and heard, "I'll be right there!" in a voice that sounded exactly like Mom Gehrig's. After waiting a few minutes for her to open the door, he realized that it was Polly playing a trick on him. He said Mom Gehrig always had to cover Polly's cage at night to get him to sleep because the bird was an expert at repeating conversations he had overheard in the exact voice of the person talking.

Pastor Ken recalled hearing stories of how covering the bird was especially important back in the days when Lou played for the Yankees because Polly was an expert at picking up foul language from Lou's fellow teammates, who were frequent visitors to the Gehrig home. I asked Ken if the bird also lived at his house, and he said Mom Gehrig kept Polly's cage on a drum table in their living room.

"Only Mom Gehrig was brave enough to stick her hand in the cage, though, because Polly was a biter," he said.

I was dying to tell Ken about seeing the bird in a cage in his childhood living room during my past-life regression, but it didn't feel like the appropriate time yet. We were both having too much fun reminiscing about Mom Gehrig.

He then told me about Mom Gehrig's dachshund by the name of Monkey, which had also taken up residence with his family. Ken recalled Mom Gehrig being a warm, loving woman, but unfortunately her dog, Monkey, wasn't quite as friendly. According to Ken, the dog would growl at anyone who tried to go near her.

"Maybe that's why people thought Mom Gehrig was stern, but I don't recall her being stern at all." Although Ken recalled Mom Gehrig speaking English well, he said she used her native German language to speak to her geriatric dachshund. He laughed with childlike exuberance when imitating how she would say, *"Essen Sie"* to get the dog to eat and *"Machen Sie schnell"* to get the dog to come.

It was as if Pastor Ken was reciting the transcripts of my past-life regression when he told me that Mom Gehrig was like a mother to his own mother, Laurel, who was 36 years her junior. Ken told me that the deep bond between the two women had been forged through their shared experience of being discriminated against by shopkeepers for their German heritage back in the days when they were neighbors and friends in New York City.

In Ken's memory, Mom Gehrig lived with his family for the last two or three years of her life. I asked Ken how old he and his sister were at the time, and he replied, "I must have been about ten when she moved in with us, which meant my sister would have been seven at the time." These were the exact ages I had reported while under hypnosis. *How could this accurate and detailed information about the children, right down to their exact ages, have possibly come through to me during my past-life regression?* Ken probably thought it was a little strange when I asked him to describe what his sister's hair looked like as a child, but I thought it was even stranger when he revealed that she had short, brown hair, just as I had described and seen so clearly in my regression.

I asked Ken if he remembered Mom Gehrig knitting, doing crossword puzzles, and reading *The New York Times*, and all answers were affirmative. He elaborated on her hobby of crocheting by sharing a funny story about finding a box with Mom Gehrig's stuff in the attic with his friends and laughing hysterically when they came upon an oversize crochet bra she had made that looked like it could hold two cannonballs. Realizing that we had been on the phone for over an hour, Ken and I mutually agreed to end our call and made a plan to speak the following week.

I knew I couldn't engage in another conversation with Reverend Ken without confessing the source of my curiosity about his surrogate grandmother, Christina Gehrig. As much as I had enjoyed hearing his colorful tales about Mom Gehrig, the time had come for me to reveal my true intentions and risk losing our budding friendship for good. Reverend Ken had already confirmed many of the details of my past-life regression without even knowing it, but I needed him to know the truth so that he could make a conscious decision to engage in further conversations or run for the hills from this crazy lady from California, the land of fruits and nuts.

For the next five days leading up to our appointed phone call, I labored over how to break the news of Christian's past-life memories and my own past-life regressions to Reverend Ken. When the time came, all my careful planning went right out the window. As soon as I heard Reverend Ken's warm greeting on the other end of the line, I blurted out, "Last week when we spoke, I told you I was writing a book about Lou and Christina Gehrig, but I was afraid to share *why* I am so interested in telling their story. What I'm about to tell you may knock your socks off . . ."

Reverend Ken patiently listened as I rattled off the sequence of events that had led me to him—Christian's past-life statements, his disdain for Babe Ruth, and meeting Dr. Tucker, who inadvertently led me to the past-life regressions with Jeroen, and right into his childhood home. The words rolled off my tongue like an elixir that would save my soul. This was the confession of a lifetime, and this Holy man on the other end of the line had somehow become critical to my salvation.

I expressed my fear of "cheating on Jesus" by even entertaining the concept of reincarnation in the first place, and I made sure he knew that Jeroen had burned sage and created a "cone of light" before our past-life regression hypnosis sessions. I shared with Pastor Ken the torment I had experienced when an e-mail from my own pastor had made me wonder if my son's body was inhabited by the spirit of a dead person.

The desperation in my voice must have sounded like an obvious cry for help. In the course of my monologue, I offered to send him the recordings and transcripts of my hypnotic regressions, and I hinted that I was hoping he could shed some light on our very peculiar situation. After finally stopping to take a breath, I asked, "So, what do you think?" I held my breath while awaiting his response.

Pastor Ken broke the silence by saying, "This is fascinating!"

"I do not believe in reincarnation due to my faith," he added, "but I do believe this is an example of wisdom and knowledge that cannot come from rational experience. It is information that comes from being in the flow of the channel of God." He continued, "This wisdom and knowledge is allowed by the Lord. It is through the will of God that this information came through from another dimension, a dimension we don't always see through our earthly eyes."

I could feel all the tension I had been carrying escape my body as I was filled with a sense of peace. Reverend Ken's words allowed me to finally let go of the battle of beliefs I had been waging in my mind for the past three and a half years. His loving words were the antidote to the fear and guilt that had burrowed their way into my heart.

When I originally called Reverend Ken, I thought my sole purpose was to find out if the details that had come up during my regression matched his recollections. I never imagined that this man would be the answer I had been searching for all along. His grace-filled words made me recognize that this journey we had been on for the past three and a half years was sacred and holy, not something to be ashamed of. I was finally able to forgive myself for "cheating on Jesus." Of course, Reverend Ken wasn't a believer in the reincarnation theory, but validation of that was not what I was seeking. I was seeking peace of mind, and I had found it in an ordinary phone call in the middle of the day while my kids were at school. I felt as if Reverend Ken was truly Heaven-sent.

Ken then explained in further detail his theory as to what Christian and I had experienced. He said he wasn't surprised by the fact that the children who experienced what Dr. Tucker refers to as past-life memories are between the ages of two and seven years old.

"This is the time when children are most in touch with the spiritual dimension that adults and school-age children are not able to see as clearly," he said. In his opinion Christian was channeling information from Lou Gehrig and I was channeling information from Mom Gehrig because these two souls were seeking completion in their relationship with each other. Choosing to believe whether it was "channeling," as Pastor Ken described or actual "past-life memories," as Dr. Tucker theorized, really did not seem necessary. All I knew for sure was that Lou Gehrig and his mother, Christina, had touched our lives in a beautiful and profound way, and I had found a new friend and mentor in Reverend Ken.

Once we concluded our deep, philosophical discussion, Ken and I went right back to laughing and reminiscing about Mom Gehrig. He said she made the best, bright-green pea soup he had ever tasted in his entire life. He was amused when I told him about my peculiar craving for pea soup when I was pregnant with Christian. Ken was able to confirm that the floor plan of the home he had lived in as a child was consistent with how I described his home while under hypnosis. It was indeed a two-story home with white siding, a gravel driveway, and a living room with windows overlooking the front yard. He said his bedroom was upstairs, just as I had reported. He didn't remember where Mom Gehrig slept, but had vivid memories of her sitting on the living room couch with her newspapers and crossword puzzles.

I saved my biggest question for last and introduced the topic by saying, "When I was speaking in the first person as Christina Gehrig during the hypnotic regression, I described jewelry my son, Lou, had given me that I wanted to give to your family." I told Ken I had specifically expressed wanting to give a necklace and charm bracelet from Japan to the little seven-year-old girl, but that I'd probably need to give it to her mother to hold on to until she was old enough. I said, "I also mentioned a watch."

Ken excitedly told me that he had indeed inherited a men's watch from Mom Gehrig that originally belonged to Lou Gehrig. He said the watch was a gift to Lou Gehrig from the Third Reich. Ken explained how he had sold some of the other items he inherited from Mom Gehrig at an auction—Lou's passport, his wedding ring, and memorabilia. He used the money to purchase his cabin on a pristine lake in New Hampshire, where he and his wife, Marilyn, spend their summers every year. Ken expressed his deep gratitude to Mom Gehrig for the watch, the cabin, and for the college scholarship she had given him when he was born in 1941, the same year that Lou Gehrig had died.

I managed to contain my utter disbelief when Pastor Ken told me that women's jewelry from Japan was among the heirlooms his family had inherited from Mom Gehrig.

"We were told that Lou bought the jewelry for his mom on a trip to Japan. My sister Jill has it now."

I was elated to hear that these items were now in the possession of Ken's sister, exactly as I had hoped for while under hypnosis. According to Pastor Ken, the jewelry had been locked up for the past 60 years in a walk-in safe that his father had built under their home because the cost of insuring the jewelry was more than his family could afford. Ken said the jewelry had remained in the safe for the most part, with the exception of a few special occasions when his mother would bring out a piece to wear while hosting dinner parties at their home. He told me nobody outside of their immediate family and a few close friends ever knew about the jewelry they had inherited from Mom Gehrig because his parents were quite discreet about it. Hearing that the jewelry I'd described while under hypnosis was actually in the possession of the Steigler family proved to me once and for all that the information coming through during my past-life regressions was anchored in reality.

As we wrapped up our conversation, Ken politely accepted my offer to e-mail him the audio recordings and transcripts of the past-life regressions. I wished him luck at the event he was planning to speak at the following day to promote interracial harmony in the Wake Forest community, and asked if he would be willing to end our phone call with a prayer. I don't recall the exact words of his blessing, but when we hung up, I felt as if I was walking on air. We carried on our conversations in the months to come and developed a sincere friendship based upon our mutual adoration and respect for Christina "Mom" Gehrig. And we always, each and every time, ended our phone calls with a prayer.

CHAPTER TWENTY-TWO

FINDING MOM GEHRIG

"There is no room in baseball for discrimination.
It is our national pastime and a game for all."

Lou Gehrig

In February 2015, nearly one full year after connecting with Reverend Ken, Christian and I took a trip to Milford, Connecticut, to visit Mom Gehrig's old stomping grounds where she had once lived with the Steigler family. As Christian and I were preparing for our trip to the East Coast, Reverend Ken and his wife, Marilyn, were preparing to attend the 50-year reunion of his historic march alongside Dr. Martin Luther King Jr. from Selma to Montgomery, Alabama, in 1965. I surmised from our conversations that the trip to Selma would be a significant pilgrimage for Ken because the graphic images of *Bloody Sunday* were forever etched in his mind. On the day that Christian and I departed for our own pilgrimage of sorts, Pastor Ken sent me an article from a North Carolina newspaper documenting his recollections of the march from Selma to Montgomery.

The article explained how 23-year-old Ken Steigler, a seminary student at the Boston University School of Theology, gathered 80 of his peers and boarded a bus headed to the Deep South to fight for the voting rights of African Americans in the midst of life-threatening social unrest. He told the reporter that the experience of personally hearing Dr. King's compassion for the adversaries of the Civil Rights Movement, even the Ku Klux Klan, had made a lasting impression on how he practices religion in his everyday life. I knew from my own interactions with Pastor Ken that a large part of his current ministry at Wake Forest United Methodist Church and All Nations Church in Raleigh was dedicated to fostering interracial harmony, a cause that has always been near and dear to my own heart as well.

When Christian and I arrived at the Hartford, Connecticut airport just before midnight, we were met with record-breaking low temperatures and no suitcase. I was a bit concerned that we had no warm clothes or jackets with us, but more distraught about being separated from the shark tooth I had packed inside of our missing suitcase for the tooth fairy to put under Christian's pillow. His wiggly tooth was hanging by a thread, and he would certainly notice if the tooth fairy forgot to give him a shark tooth in exchange for his own—a long-standing family tradition. I was touched by the generosity of a woman in the baggage claim area who gifted me with a down jacket off of her back when she noticed our luggage was nowhere to be found. Her gesture inspired another man standing nearby to wrap a warm blanket around Christian, who had convinced me to let him wear shorts for the trip to chilly

Connecticut. It was the first time I found myself longing for the days of the recent past when our son used to insist upon wearing baseball pants every day. He still refused to wear long pants unless they were baseball pants, but he had added shorts to his wardrobe choices shortly after his fifth birthday. The jacketless woman then whispered into my ear, "I don't know what your religious beliefs are, but Jesus loves you." And with that, this earth angel disappeared into a flurry of snow.

After a good night's sleep and a shopping spree sponsored by American Airlines, Christian and I made the one-hour drive to Milford, Connecticut to visit Reverend Ken's childhood home, the home where Mom Gehrig had lived with his family during the final years of her life. Just as we were approaching our destination, Christian yelled, "Hey, look, a snowman family!" Sensing his excitement, I pulled over to give him an up-close-and-personal view of the festive creatures made out of snow. I asked Christian if he remembered building a snowman on our family ski trip to Mammoth Mountain when he was three. I was surprised when he said he had no recollection of ever having been in the snow before. As he smiled for a photo with the four snow creatures, he said, "They have four people in their family just like us, but Lou Gehrig had only three people in his family." I had always made a point of never telling Christian the details of Lou Gehrig's life, so I was surprised when he correctly stated that Lou Gehrig was an only child. I chuckled to myself at the irony of Christian remembering things from another person's lifetime, but not being able to recall moments from his own life.

Even though the Steiglers' former home was only a couple of doors down from our snowman adventure, I opted to drive the short distance, due to the blankets of snow falling from the sky. Everything about the two-story home looked remarkably familiar: the white siding I had seen so clearly under hypnosis, the gravel driveway where I said I had parked my car, and the large picture window I had described looking out of while sitting on the couch in the living room. In my mind's eye, I saw Mom Gehrig sitting on the couch inside doing crossword puzzles, knitting, and reading *The New York Times*—activities Reverend Ken had confirmed she loved to do. Standing in the front yard of my personal historic landmark felt like a homecoming of sorts. We didn't bother knocking on the door because the next-door neighbor who saw us standing in front of the home informed us that the owners were out of town for the weekend.

Our next stop was the snow-covered Little League fields where, during my past-life regression, I had described Mom Gehrig bringing cookies to the boys, the same fields where she had watched Pastor Ken play baseball more than 60 years before. Behind the backstop of the snow-covered field was a plaque honoring Christina "Mom" Gehrig that was dated 1954, the year of her death. Prior to our trip to Connecticut, I had contacted the president of Lou Gehrig Little League in Milford to see if he might be able to help me track down anybody in town who had played baseball in the league during the early 1950s when Mom Gehrig lived in Milford.

I told him I was hoping to interview Little League players who had actually met Mom Gehrig for a book I was writing. "They're probably in their seventies by now," I explained. The Little League president didn't know of any offhand, but he referred me to Coach Kipp Taylor, who was the resident expert on Mom Gehrig's history in the small, seaside town.

"Coach Kipp was single-handedly responsible for preserving the memory of Lou and Mom Gehrig in the local community," he added, "when he convinced the league not to drop the *Lou Gehrig* from its name a few years back."

My call to Coach Kipp revealed that, in addition to being a youth baseball coach for many years, Kipp had also served as the president of Lou Gehrig Little League for several years, a generous act of kindness made even grander by the fact that Kipp didn't have any kids of his own. Fifty-year-old Kipp was far too young to have met Mom Gehrig himself, but his love and respect for this woman came shining through in every word he spoke of her. I had miraculously found someone who was as enamored with Mom Gehrig as I was. Kipp told me how he had recently taken it upon himself to repaint the plaque honoring Mom Gehrig that Christian and I had seen at the Lou Gehrig Little League field because the inscription was becoming difficult to read. A few days before our trip to Connecticut, Kipp had surprised me with the good news that he'd found a 75-year-old former Little League player named Ken Hawkins, who was willing to meet with us.

I met Kipp at the Milford Public Library on a Tuesday evening at 5 so we could get acquainted before Mr. Hawkins was scheduled to join us. When Christian and I walked into the library, an upbeat man with deep dimples and a contagious smile approached us.

"Hi, are you Cathy and Christian?" He introduced himself as Coach Kipp, a nickname that has stuck to him like glue from his many years of coaching and teaching.

We went upstairs to find a secluded meeting area where we'd be able to talk without bothering others who had come to this landmark in the center of town for quieter escapades. Christian played baseball games on his iPad while Coach Kipp shared the numerous news clippings on Mom Gehrig he had printed from microfiche a few years back when he was trying to convince the Little League board of directors not to drop *Lou Gehrig* from the league's name. In what felt like only a few minutes but was probably closer to an hour, Kipp's phone rang, and he excused himself to fetch Ken Hawkins from the library lobby.

When Ken Hawkins entered the room with Kipp, I stood to shake his hand and was immediately struck by his charismatic yet soft-spoken demeanor. We exchanged business cards and found it amusing that we were both residential real estate brokers. Coach Kipp and I were shocked when Ken started the conversation by saying, "My family was quite close with Mom Gehrig . . ."

Mr. Hawkins elaborated by telling us that Mom Gehrig and his father, Ellsworth, were very good friends and founders of the local Little League together. Coach Kipp and I looked at each other and our jaws dropped in unison—this was a brand-new revelation.

This former Little League All-Star told us that Mom Gehrig was a fixture in the stands at the Little League fields. Ken reminisced about Mom Gehrig.

"She didn't miss a single Little League game until the day she passed. Nothing made her happier than a day at the baseball field."

Ken opened a file he had brought along with him and handed us an article that listed his father, Ellsworth Hawkins, among the pallbearers at Christina Gehrig's funeral. The article read:

And at the expressed wish of this woman to whom the words "batter up!" were symbolic of her greatest enthusiasm, many of her friends have donated money to Little League instead of sending flowers to her funeral.

As Ken kept pulling out news clippings and photographs, Coach Kipp and I were like kids in a candy shop. Even Christian was intrigued enough by our conversation to look away from his iPad while Ken Hawkins was speaking about Mom Gehrig.

Also among the articles was a photo of Mom Gehrig and Ken's father, Ellsworth Hawkins, at a ceremony to rename the league *Lou Gehrig Little League* in 1952. Another news clipping stated that Mom Gehrig had willed $500 to the league upon her death. The article said Mrs. Gehrig had served on the board of directors since the inception of the league and "never missed a ball game." My favorite article of all was a story about little Kenny Hawkins stepping to the plate with the bases loaded during the final inning of the District Championship All-Star game in 1951. The article described Kenny taking two strikes and then smashing a long, high home run over the fence to win the game. Ken Hawkins shared his memory of Mom Gehrig sitting in the stands that day and cheering his team to victory.

Like Reverend Ken, Ken Hawkins also had the unique experience of being Mom Gehrig's guest at New York Yankees games when he was a child.

"Mrs. Gehrig was probably the most famous mom in Major League Baseball," said Ken.

He told us how the Yankees players were so excited to see her at the ballpark before the game that they hopped the fence behind their dugout to shower her with hugs. Mr. Hawkins said Mom Gehrig was "Mom" to everyone who knew her and even those who didn't. He also recalled never being hungry when Mom Gehrig was around.

"She always brought a big picnic basket filled with sandwiches and other goodies she had prepared herself," he said with a smile.

When the time came for us to go our separate ways, Ken Hawkins gifted me with a folder filled with the articles, a copy of Lou Gehrig's 1933 contract with the New York Yankees, and a photo of Babe Ruth and Lou Gehrig that Mom Gehrig had personally signed to him. The three of us reflected on the irony of Mom Gehrig's legacy to Little League, given that she initially wanted her son to give up baseball to attend college and become an engineer. Ken told us that Mom Gehrig had donated a plaque made of Vermont granite in honor of Milford Little League being renamed for Lou Gehrig on June 29, 1952, two years prior to her death. He said the dedication was a celebrated affair and attended by the commissioner of Major League Baseball, Ford Frick, and by the founder of Little League Baseball, Carl E. Stotz.

When the time came to say good-bye, I gave Ken a hug and said, "I bet you were Mom Gehrig's favorite." I was surprised by the words that came out of my mouth, but I somehow knew it to be true. Ken's boyish grin made me feel as if I was Mom Gehrig for a moment—speaking to a dear friend who was much younger than me. Driving back to our hotel that night, I wondered if Ken Hawkins could be the other young boy I had described in my final past-life regression.

Our suitcase finally showed up at our hotel one day before our scheduled departure back to Los Angeles and, as luck would have it, Christian's wiggly tooth chose the same day to fall out. He had been asking me all week if the tooth fairy would be able to find him to bring him a shark tooth in Connecticut, and thankfully she was. That afternoon I reached into the pocket of the down jacket that had been keeping me warm for the past week and was ecstatic to find a paycheck stub with a phone number written on it. When I dialed the number, the friendly voice on the other end of the line informed me that she was the sister of the woman whose name was on the paycheck stub. When I told her that I would like to mail the jacket back to her sister and thank her for the kind gesture, she confirmed that the address on the paycheck was the correct mailing address. After a stop at the post office to mail the jacket with a thank-you note, my mission felt complete.

On our way to the airport, we squeezed in a visit to the Gehrig home at 9 Meadow Lane in New Rochelle, New York. The first thing I noticed when we drove up to the home we had toured the previous summer was a *For Sale* sign in the snow-covered yard. Our knock on the front door was greeted by big hugs from Jimmy and Marisol, who invited us in and shared the news that they were about to sign off on an offer to short sale their home. I was concerned when I looked up the prices of comparable homes in the neighborhood that had recently sold and found that Jimmy and Marisol were potentially selling their home at half of the current market value. I knew that Jimmy was on disability and unable to work because of an injury, so I offered to assist them with applying for a loan modification to help them keep their home. I hoped their own real estate agent would understand that it was not in the best interests of her clients or the bank holding the large mortgage to sell the home at $300,000 below the market value—especially this beautiful home that Lou Gehrig was so proud of.

"I saw this house in September 1927," Lou said to a reporter. "I fell in love with it right then. It was my kind of house. Look at those trees, real big ones, real forest trees. They're bigger even than the ones you see in Central Park. It's got eight or nine rooms, three floors, and a basement. I tell you it's just what I've always wanted."

Our time in Connecticut further strengthened the bond I felt with Mom Gehrig, as if she'd become my own family. Mom Gehrig, I knew, was a true hero in the face of adversity. During my regressions, I had felt the deep sense of loss she had experienced after the death of her son. I now also felt the love she had for the baseball boys up until the last day of her life and the joy she had discovered through her advocacy for youth baseball. I knew in my heart that Mom Gehrig loved being at every Little League game as much as the boys loved having her there. My otherworldly encounter with this woman, who had passed away 13 years prior to my own birth, cemented my belief in the eternity of the soul and proved to me that love can surpass one lifetime.

CHAPTER TWENTY-THREE

108 STITCHES

"We shall not cease from exploration
And the end of all our exploring
Will be to arrive where we started
And know the place for the first time."

T. S. ELIOT, "LITTLE GIDDING"

Our return to sunny Southern California was a welcome relief from the subzero temperatures of the East Coast. After being delayed one extra day by a tempestuous winter storm, Christian and I made it back home the night before what had become my favorite day of the year, Little League Opening Day. Ever since the very first Little League game in 1939, a trip to the ballpark has been something akin to a religious experience for young kids playing a grown-up's game. Today was no different. Now six years old, Christian was about to embark on his fourth season of participating in this rite of passage. For parents and children alike, the new Little League season's fresh start stirs hopeful anticipation of what lies ahead. This spring Christian would be donning a black jersey emblazoned with big, orange letters that spelled the word *Giants* across his chest—somewhat of a sin for a loyal Dodgers fan, but he wore it with pride knowing that his teammates would be doing the same.

Getting a family of four dressed and out the door before eight o'clock on a Saturday morning is never an easy task, but the fact that I had gained three hours when we arrived back in town the night before was working in my favor. While Christian sat in his regular shoe-tying spot on the bottom step of our staircase, I double knotted his cleats and read him a text that Coach Kipp had sent earlier that morning.

"Please tell Christian to have a great day and remember to play fair, play hard, never quit, and always have fun."

I hoped Kipp's encouraging words would ease Christian's apprehensions of playing in the Kid Pitch Division with players who were up to three years older than him.

During our short drive to the baseball fields, Christian told us that he wasn't nervous at all about pitching to third-graders; but he was petrified of being hit by a ball thrown by the opposing pitchers who would be much older and stronger than him. Michael, Charlotte, Christian, and I enjoyed a pre-ceremony pancake breakfast put on by the local Rotary Club, and then we made our way to the professional photographer's booth, where we met up with Christian's team for a group photo.

After breakfast we walked over to the main field where hundreds of Little League players between the ages of 4 and 13 were assembling in preparation for the opening ceremony. Christian and I sat with his Giants team while Charlotte and Michael looked on from the stands. The buzz of the crowd's excited chatter was silenced when the league president stepped up to the microphone at home plate to address the crowd. Following his lead, the boys removed their hats and placed them over their hearts as the national anthem played over the makeshift sound system. When the anthem was over, the league president introduced National Baseball Hall of Fame manager Tommy Lasorda.

Applause and cheers filled the air as Tommy walked to the microphone to address the crowd. Even the kids who didn't recognize him sensed that this was a special moment from the looks of awe on the faces of their parents and coaches.

"I believe that God put every one of us on earth to help others," Tommy said. "Baseball is a game of helping others, of coming together; you can't win it alone. Baseball is a community game; you need nine people helping one another. You can be the best pitcher in all of baseball, but somebody has to get you a run to win the game. I love the idea of a sacrifice bunt—giving yourself up for the good of the whole. You find your own good in the good of the whole. You find your own individual fulfillment in the success of the community."

Tommy was serious, and looked into the kids' faces when he said:

"You hold the future of our country in your hands. While you're out there on the field with your teammates playing this beautiful game, you're learning skills that will serve you for the rest of your life. You're learning how to follow directions, how to get along with other people, and how to play by the rules."

Tommy wrapped up his touching speech by saying, "Respect your parents, especially your mothers, who make everything possible."

Christian glanced at me with a smile and I gave his shoulders a squeeze. Meanwhile, Tommy brought that point home:

"The two things you owe your parents are love and respect," he told them, and then asked them all loudly:

"What do you owe your parents?"

When the response wasn't loud enough, Tommy said, "I can't hear you. What do you owe your parents?"

The crowd roared in unison, "LOVE AND RESPECT!"

Satisfied with the response, Tommy handed the microphone back to the Little League president, who recited the Little League pledge.

"I trust in God. I love my country and will respect its laws. I will play fair and strive to win, but win or lose, I will always do my best."

Before it was over, another voice bellowed out from the loudspeakers—a voice that had become as familiar to our family as that of a close friend.

"I have been walking on ball fields for sixteen years . . ." said the voice of Lou Gehrig in a crackling recording from his retirement speech at Yankee Stadium that memorable day in 1939.

Christian looked at me with eyes as big as saucers as soon as we heard Lou's voice.

". . . and I've never received anything but kindness and encouragement from you fans. When you have a father and a mother who work all their lives so you can have an education and build your body—it's a blessing. For the past two weeks, you have been reading about a bad break I got. Today I consider myself the luckiest man on the face of the Earth. And I might have been given a bad break, but I've got an awful lot to live for."

Could this really be happening? Christian reflected my thoughts when he said, "I can't believe it!" He scooted over to sit on my lap and I wrapped my arms tightly around him. The significance of the moment was not lost on either of us.

As the crowd dispersed, we walked to the field where Christian's first game of the season was about to begin. Tommy Lasorda joined us in the stands where we sat with family and friends, including my mom, her boyfriend Dennis, and Aunt Cinthia. Christian's team would be facing my least favorite coach—the one whose son had mowed Christian down during a game, resulting in a neck injury. As that coach walked toward first base, we made eye contact. I smiled at him and waved—feeling inspired by Tommy's heart-touching speech. The coach surprised me by cracking a smile in return. With that simple gesture, my grudge toward the man disappeared.

Christian stepped onto the mound, and as he hurled the first pitch, my heart overflowed with gratitude. It was obvious that everything I had been searching for was right in front of me. I realized that there is no greater pleasure than sharing the highs and lows of the passing seasons with our family and friends. The battle fought and the lessons learned are far more significant than the victory, and a new season's fresh start is always right around the corner, whether it be in sports or in life.

Perhaps it is no accident that a baseball has 108 stitches and a prayer necklace has 108 beads. Baseball does not discriminate, and we do not have to believe in the same God to be on the same team. It is a game of courage, strength, and character that can bring grown men to cry. As easy as it appears, it is heartbreakingly difficult. Anyone who has ever stood behind the plate knows there are no guarantees that your preparation, hard work, and perseverance will be rewarded, but without them you will surely strike out. Baseball is a game that embraces failure, an arena where striking out two-thirds of the time is considered success. Former Yankees manager Joe Torre frequently reminded his players of his own experiences with failure. He told them about the season when his batting average dropped by 90 points, just one year after earning the batting title, and how he once batted into four double plays in a single game. To fail is human, but making the choice to get back up again after failing is superhuman.

I never imagined that becoming a mother would send me to the heights of wonder and propel me into the abyss of my own limitations as a parent and as a human being. I've learned that living a spiritual life isn't necessarily about sitting on a yoga mat, or in church, or in a temple. Those things are nice and they can help us find balance, but it's about much more than that. It is about reaching deep within ourselves to find the courage to forgive and act with compassion and kindness, even in those moments when we find ourselves sitting across from someone who has activated those dark places within us that make us want to cause them pain. Living a spiritual life is about being on a Little League baseball field, watching someone intentionally hurt our child, and responding to the situation with love rather than anger. I'm not saying that we should put a child in danger, or roll over and let other people use us as a doormat, but by honoring ourselves and others, in good times and bad, is how we can truly make a difference and let our own light shine while helping others to shine a little brighter too. It was never really about baseball after all. It was about a game called life.

EPILOGUE

A WINK FROM THE UNIVERSE

"A life is not important, except in the
impact it has on other lives."

JACKIE ROBINSON

Two years have passed since that Little League opening day in 2015. It seemed like an appropriate place to end our story because it marked the beginning of a new chapter of our lives—one where Christian's spontaneous recollections of his life as Lou Gehrig were becoming a distant memory. It was as if the Angel Lailah finally showed up and ushered him into a new life unencumbered by memories of the past by pressing on his upper lip and whispering, "shhh."

In the spring of 2015, Christian and I had a meeting with a movie producer at Sony Pictures, who had heard about our story from a mutual friend. After quizzing Christian about Lou Gehrig, the producer asked, "Is Lou

Gehrig still alive today?" Everyone in the room, including me, was surprised when Christian confidently replied, "Yes." The producer carried on a playful exchange with Christian while the rest of us silently observed.

"Where is he?"

"Here."

"Where here? Like in this room here?"

Christian nodded, slipped his right hand down the neckline of his shirt to place his hand on his bare chest, and said, "In my heart."

These three words perfectly sum up how our lives have been touched by Lou and Christina Gehrig to this day. Christian still keeps the photo of Lou and Mom Gehrig on the bookshelf beside his bed and Charlotte still teases him about Babe Ruth. Lou and Christina Gehrig have become honorary members of our family and our affection for them is much like the feelings we have for our loved ones who have passed away. The connection will always be there, even though their physical presence is missed.

In the summer of 2015, I returned to Cooperstown, New York, with Charlotte and Christian for two weeks at Cooperstown Baseball Camp with the Cepedas. My nagging urge to scour the Gehrig family documents had disappeared along with Christian's past-life memories. Our story was complete and our only trip to the National Baseball Hall of Fame Library during that trip was to attend Tommy Lasorda's book signing, followed by lunch with our favorite Hall of Famer. Tommy had become a fixture at Christian's All-Star games that summer and his dugout pep talks delighted the parents and kids alike.

As we were exiting the National Baseball Hall of Fame, Uncle Tommy stopped in front of three life-size bronze statues in the lobby. On the wall next to the statues was a placard that read, "Character and Courage." Tommy read the names of the three men aloud to Charlotte and Christian, "Lou Gehrig, Roberto Clemente, and Jackie Robinson." He said, "You see these three men? Their statues are the first thing you see when you walk into the Hall of Fame. You know why?" After a pause, Tommy said, "Because in addition to being three of the greatest ballplayers of all time, these men demonstrated courage and character—on and off the field. Character means treating people the way you'd like to be treated. That means showing respect for *all* people, having the courage to stand up for what's right and speak out against what's wrong." Tommy's speech that day further deepened our respect and admiration for Lou Gehrig and Tommy.

During that two-week trip to the East Coast in the summer of 2015, we made a road trip to New Hampshire to meet Pastor Ken and his lovely wife, Marilyn, who were staying at their summer home. I was excited to finally meet Ken in person and see the cottage he had purchased with the proceeds of the family heirlooms Mom Gehrig had bequeathed to him. It was easy to spot Pastor Ken at the lakeside restaurant where we met because of the clergy collar he wore under his blue button-down shirt. The connection I felt to this kindhearted man was immediate and we laughed when he commented that the crocheted shirt I was wearing reminded him of something Mom Gehrig would have made.

Our lunch was followed by a stop at the local creamery for the best ice-cream cones I've ever tasted, a round of miniature golf, and a game of baseball at a secret field in the woods designed to look like a mini Fenway Park. Christian immediately noticed the similarity of the towering CITGO sign behind the large green outfield wall to the field he had played on during the filming of *That's My Boy*. Christian and Charlotte took turns hitting while Pastor Ken played catcher. Our visit culminated with a tour of Ken and Marilyn's charming cottage perched on a hill with sweeping views of the picturesque tree-lined lake, conveniently located next to the Alton Bay Christian Conference Center, where Ken serves as a guest pastor in the summertime. We will long remember Ken and Marilyn's gracious hospitality, and Charlotte will never let us forget who won at mini-golf.

We ended our East Coast trip that summer with a barbecue at 9 Meadow Lane in New Rochelle, New York—the home Lou Gehrig had purchased in 1927 when he signed his first big contract with the Yankees. Our friends Jimmy and Marisol, the current owners of the home, invited their friends and family for a celebration in honor of our visit. It was a surreal experience to sit in the backyard eating and conversing while Charlotte and Christian climbed trees and squirted each other with a hose. The scene seemed somehow familiar and reminiscent of the entertaining that Mom Gehrig was so well known for during her days in that home nearly a century ago.

I returned to Cooperstown, New York, in the summer of 2016 with the intention of finishing this book. I rented an air-conditioned camper at the Cooperstown Baseball Camp for the entire month of July for a mere $400 per week—the cost of one night at a motel in Cooperstown during the very popular National Baseball Hall of Fame induction weekend. Christian, Michael, and Charlotte stayed behind in Southern California to watch Christian's All-Star baseball team win their way to the PONY World Series for seven-year-olds, while I spent 10–16 hours per day writing in my camper in the woods. Christian and his teammate Ayden accomplished the very rare feat of pitching a perfect game during their team's 39-game run to the World Series that summer. Following the final game, Christian joined me in New York to attend Cooperstown Baseball Camp for the last two weeks of July and I miraculously managed to finish my manuscript on the very last day of our trip. I had hoped to take him to a Yankees game while we were in New York, but the pressure of my impending deadline kept me glued to my computer day and night.

We checked in for our flight at the Albany airport with the intention of returning to Los Angeles, but God had other plans for us. Our flight to Charlotte for our connection to LAX had been canceled due to an approaching thunderstorm. The gate agent said I would need to get a hotel room at my own expense and come back in the morning. At that exact moment, a couple at the counter next to us was checking in for a flight to Tampa Bay, Florida—the last flight scheduled to depart the Albany airport that day. A quick Google search on my phone revealed that a hotel room in Tampa Bay would be half the cost of hotel room in Albany, so I said to the gate agent who was assisting us, "Is there any chance you can reroute us through Tampa Bay?" Sure enough, we found ourselves on a plane headed to Tampa Bay with a connecting flight to Los Angeles first thing the following morning. Our hotel shuttle driver noticed Christian decked out in baseball gear and said, "You know, the Yankees are in town this weekend to play the Tampa Bay Rays. Last game of the series is tomorrow, and there are always plenty of tickets available." Christian's face lit up with a wide smile. "Mommy, can we please go?"

By the time we arrived at our hotel it was nearly midnight, and Christian fell asleep right away. My 4 A.M. wake-up call came in what seemed like the blink of an eye. Rather than hopping in the shower to get ready to go back to the airport, I decided to call the airline to ask if we might be able to delay our flight by a day to go to the game. When Christian woke up a few hours later I surprised him with the news that we would be seeing the Yankees play the Tampa Bay Rays instead of flying home. I'd never seen him quite so excited about anything in his life. He started naming all of the players from both teams and their positions—a skill he had acquired from many hours of playing virtual baseball on his PlayStation MLB video game. As we hopped into our Uber car, Christian said, "Dear God—please let me meet Evan Longoria from the Rays!"

The Uber driver was unable to drive us to the main gate of the stadium because it was blocked off to traffic, so he dropped us off at a side entrance. As we walked into the air-conditioned concourse of the indoor stadium, the first thing we saw was a large framed photograph of Lou Gehrig that was being raffled off for charity. Of course, I couldn't resist entering the drawing to tempt fate. What happened next is a moment that neither of us will ever forget. As we walked to our seats, a video of Lou Gehrig giving his "Luckiest Man" speech appeared on the big screen. A man at a podium near home plate recited the words of Lou Gehrig's familiar speech and it quickly became apparent that we had just walked into a pregame presentation honoring Lou Gehrig for ALS Awareness Day. Here we were, in a city that we were not supposed to be in, preparing to see a Yankees game, and a video of Lou Gehrig was playing on the big screen. I immediately took out my video camera and began filming so I could prove to myself that it wasn't a dream.

When the pregame ceremony concluded, we walked down to the dugout to get a closer view of the players as they were warming up on the field. Out of nowhere came a man who introduced Christian to the Tampa Bay Rays' star player Evan Longoria—the same Evan Longoria who Christian was hoping and praying to meet. The man handed me his business card, which said he held the Guinness World Record for owning the largest collection of autographed baseballs—more than 4,400 balls in total. Christian asked, "Do you have any balls signed by Lou Gehrig?" The man answered right away, "I sure do. I have four balls signed by Lou Gehrig." Just then, Evan Longoria came up to where we were standing, and I shot a video of him signing a ball and tossing it to Christian. This was quickly turning into the best day of Christian's life to date. I'm sure it is no surprise to hear that we ended up winning the framed photo of Lou Gehrig, and after the game Christian and I posed for a picture holding our prized Lou Gehrig photo in front of the Yankees dugout. I consider our memorable day at the ballpark a wink from the universe.

The timing of this particular wink from the universe was not lost on me. You see, ever since embarking on the journey of deciding to share our story with the world, I had struggled—really struggled—with whether or not I was making the right decision. I knew from the start that writing this book could potentially hurt the people I care about most. I worried endlessly about the negative effects it could have on Charlotte and Christian in their day-to-day lives. This fateful day in Tampa Bay felt like validation that I was on the right path. My fears melted away, and from that day forward I focused on how people's lives might be touched in a positive way by reading our story. It is my hope that after reading this book people will be inspired to love a little more, judge a little less, and treasure the adventure of living each day to the fullest. I never found an explanation as to why a baseball has 108 stitches and why a prayer necklace has 108 beads, but I did celebrate when the Chicago Cubs won the World Series for the first time in 108 years. What I know for sure is all that truly matters in this lifetime is the difference we make in the lives of others.

Love is the answer, always.

ACKNOWLEDGMENTS

"Pay attention to synchronicities and people
who touch your life every day. These people can
be angels who will help you along the way."

Dr. Wayne Dyer

There are three special people, earth angels really, without whom this book would not exist. They are Karin Gutman, Mira Kelley, and Dr. Wayne Dyer.

My first word of thanks goes to Karin Gutman, my writing guru. Responding to Karin's ad on jenslist.com for a writing workshop called *Unlocking Your Story* in the summer of 2014 was perhaps the most life-changing decision of my life. The workshop promised to "unleash the stories that reflect the uniqueness of your personal journey," and that it did. My heartfelt thanks also goes out to my incredibly talented classmates who helped me find my voice as a writer and muster the courage to share our story with the world. It was also Karin who suggested that I attend the Hay House Writer's Workshop in Maui that ultimately led to me winning a book publishing contest.

The second ray of light to waltz into my life at precisely the right moment was Hay House author and past-life regression therapist Mira Kelley. Mira seems to have a direct line to the Divine, and she was instrumental in bringing our story to the attention of Dr. Wayne Dyer. In January 2015, Mira came to our home in Southern California and did a past-life regression session with Christian to help him release his ties to Lou Gehrig. Since Mira's visit, Christian has not made a single trip to the doctor for breathing treatments. This is one of the greatest gifts of all to come out of our journey to the past. A special thanks also goes out to Mira's assistant Tamra Edgar for her love and support every step of the way.

The third magical being who was instrumental in bringing this book to life is no longer with us in his physical body, but I've felt his presence more than ever in the miracles and synchronicities that continue to unfold around our story. I met Dr. Wayne Dyer in Maui at the Hay House Writer's Workshop in June 2015, just two months prior to his passing. At the time, he and his co-writer, Dee Garnes, were putting the finishing touches on their book *Memories of Heaven: Children's Astounding Recollections of the Time Before They Came to Earth*. It was Wayne's enthusiasm for our story that inspired Reid Tracy and Patty Gift at Hay House to take a chance on me as a first-time author with no existing platform.

I like to refer to my friends who have been there for me at every turn on the road to publishing this book as my book angels. The condensed version of this list consists of my insightful publicist Elizabeth Much and my pals Christopher Broughton, DeVon Franklin, Cinthia Dahl, Mela Conway Breijo, Kathryn Werner, Melissa Oppenheimer Friedman, Lisa Fugard, Natasha Stoynoff, Shirley Brooke, Brigitte Perreault, Catherine Sarah Manna, Lon Rosen, Rachel Rose Brekke, Alvin and Gwen Clayton, Kimberly Ruic, Elizabeth McDonnell, Betsy Michaud, Julie Rodriguez, Maria Sprowl, Angelo Anastasio, Alina Shalev, Leon

Capetanos, Rhonda Finkel, Ann Bucklin, Gary Hudson, Hillary Bibicoff, Geoff Nathanson, Stacy Morgan-Kaine, Steve Lyons, Kathee Wilson, Kajsa Garrett, Steph Arnold, Beth Bell, Zhena Muzyka, Mikki Willis, Patty Aubrey, Tammy Anczok, Genta Luddy, Lynda Huey, Dee Garnes, Michael Levine, Serena Dyer, and Zoe Kors.

I will never forget the Yoga Barn in Ubud, Bali, where I spent a month writing my first draft in the company of 30 writers equally committed to illuminating the world with light and love. I am especially grateful to my Bali Scribtribe sisters Satchi Royers, Jodie Jaimes, Katie Rudman, and to our fabulous host Alit "Agung" Sumerta. A big thanks also goes to our German exchange student, Max Lorenz, who kept Charlotte and Christian entertained while I was away.

I'm especially grateful for all of the wonderful youth baseball coaches who have nurtured Christian's love for the game. Nick Koep—you get the number one accolade for being his primary coach and mentor for three straight years. The countless hours you've spent working with Christian on and off the field are priceless, but I appreciate you most for always keeping it fun. A word of acknowledgment also goes to Coach Jay Lucas and his superhuman baseball mom wife, Kirsten, who coined the phrase, "Who cares about baseball, we're training young men here!" And to all of the fantastic baseball families we've come to know and love over the years—that includes you, Harris "Pop" Steinberg.

I could have never completed this book without the unwavering support of my real estate clients, who beared with me when my publishing deadlines were requiring the majority of my attention—especially Grace and Masaki Matsuo whose escrows fell in to the thick of my final deadline. I'm also incredibly grateful to my COMPASS real estate colleagues and to our fearless leaders Robert Reffkin, Jay Rubenstein, and Kathy Mehringer.

My greatest respect and admiration goes to the extraordinary people at Hay House, the only publishing house I ever wanted to partner with. I am grateful for the love and creative touch of the entire Hay House team, especially my gifted editor Sally Mason-Swaab. Thank you for being champions for my book: Patty Gift, Reid Tracy, Stacey Smith, Stacy Horowitz, Richelle Fredson, Marlene Robinson, and Jo Burgess. My heartfelt thanks also goes to 99designs.com for the original cover design and to Tricia Breidenthal for the new and improved version. The artistic contributions of Pamela Homan and Caroline DiNofia are also much appreciated. And to sweet Diane Thomas, we must have broken some kind of record for the most photo licenses and releases in a single book.

To all of the people who have graciously allowed me write about how they have touched our lives: thank you, for without your support, there would be no story to tell. This list of real-life superheroes includes Dr. Jim B. Tucker, Tommy Lasorda, Reverend Kenneth and Marilyn Steigler, Jeroen de Wit, Kenneth B. Hawkins, Carol Bowman, Jimmy Fizzinoglia, Marisol Lopez, Coach Kipp Taylor, Rhiannon Potkey, Tracy Lappin, my cousin Leanne Woehlke (Epic Yoga), my sister Laura Hickman (and her mother Sonia Byrd), Joe McDonnell, Ben Maller, Debbie Tate-Baltau (Mrs. B), Adam Sandler, Jessi Moore, Kevin Grady, Dennis Foley, Ali and Malcolm Cepeda, Juli and Dwaine Sharratt, Matt Rothenberg, and John Horne. Mark J. Terrill, Jon SooHoo, and Ed Lobenhofer—thank you for so beautifully capturing the timeless photos of Christian's first pitch at Dodger Stadium. I am also grateful for the help of the National

Baseball Hall of Fame, the Los Angeles Dodgers, Wilson Sporting Goods, and Major League Baseball.

Jack Canfield—your generosity of spirit blows me away, and you continue to inspire me on a daily basis. Thank you for believing in me more than I believed in myself. You and your phenomenal team showed up in my life at just the right time. I am also thankful to the light-workers, who found time in their busy schedules to read a book from an unknown author, and offer their words of support. Thank you Dr. Eben Alexander, Karen Newell, John Gray, Dr. Brian L. Weiss, Michael Bernard Beckwith, Mike Dooley, Dr. Shefali Tsabary, Robert Holden, James Van Praagh, Mira Kelley, Elliot Mintz, Mark Langill, and Tommy Lasorda.

To my parents, Judy and Richard Byrd—any good I've ever done in the world is because of you. Thank you for being my guiding light. To Michael—thank you for allowing me to fulfill my lifelong dream of becoming a mother and for inspiring me to spread my wings and fly. Charlotte and Christian—my love for you has no limits. Thank you for the gift of being your mom and for the inimitable joy you bring to my life. I will always be your biggest fan.

I am eternally grateful to God above, the master creator of this great adventure we call life.

ABOUT THE AUTHOR

Cathy Byrd is a residential real estate broker and mother of two young children who never had aspirations of becoming a writer until her three-year-old son began sharing memories of being a baseball player in the 1920s and '30s. A Southern California native, Cathy received her B.A. from UCLA and her M.B.A. from Pepperdine University. Prior to becoming a Realtor, Cathy had an exciting 10-year career in sports marketing, working for the World Cup and Olympic Torch Relay Organizing Committees and serving as vice president of the Magic Johnson Foundation. The most likely place to find Cathy in her free time is at a youth baseball field.

To learn more and access the full regression transcripts, visit: cathy-byrd.com

HAY HOUSE TITLES OF RELATED INTEREST

YOU CAN HEAL YOUR LIFE, the movie,
starring Louise Hay & Friends
(available as a 1-DVD program and an expanded 2-DVD set)
Watch the trailer at: www.LouiseHayMovie.com

THE SHIFT, the movie,
starring Dr. Wayne W. Dyer
(available as a 1-DVD program and an expanded 2-DVD set)
Watch the trailer at: www.DyerMovie.com

*BEYOND PAST LIVES: What Parallel Realities Can Teach Us about
Relationships, Healing, and Transformation,* by Mira Kelley

*MIRRORS OF TIME: Using Regression for Physical, Emotional, and
Spiritual Healing,* by Brian L. Weiss, M.D.

*MEMORIES OF HEAVEN: Children's Astounding
Recollections of the Time Before They Came to Earth,*
by Dr. Wayne W. Dyer and Dee Garnes

*SAVED BY AN ANGEL: True Accounts of People Who Have Had
Extraordinary Experiences with Angels . . . and How YOU Can, Too!*
by Doreen Virtue

All of the above are available at your local bookstore,
or may be ordered by visiting:

Hay House USA: www.hayhouse.com®
Hay House Australia: www.hayhouse.com.au
Hay House UK: www.hayhouse.co.uk
Hay House South Africa: www.hayhouse.co.za
Hay House India: www.hayhouse.co.in

We hope you enjoyed this Hay House book. If you'd like to receive our online catalog featuring additional information on Hay House books and products, or if you'd like to find out more about the Hay Foundation, please contact:

Hay House, Inc., P.O. Box 5100, Carlsbad, CA 92018-5100
(760) 431-7695 or (800) 654-5126
(760) 431-6948 (fax) or (800) 650-5115 (fax)
www.hayhouse.com® • www.hayfoundation.org

Published and distributed in Australia by:
Hay House Australia Pty. Ltd., 18/36 Ralph St., Alexandria NSW 2015
Phone: 612-9669-4299 • *Fax:* 612-9669-4144 • www.hayhouse.com.au

Published and distributed in the United Kingdom by: Hay House UK, Ltd.,
Astley House, 33 Notting Hill Gate, London W11 3JQ
Phone: 44-20-3675-2450 • *Fax:* 44-20-3675-2451 • www.hayhouse.co.uk

Published and distributed in the Republic of South Africa by:
Hay House SA (Pty), Ltd., P.O. Box 990, Witkoppen 2068
info@hayhouse.co.za • www.hayhouse.co.za

Published in India by: Hay House Publishers India,
Muskaan Complex, Plot No. 3, B-2, Vasant Kunj, New Delhi 110 070
Phone: 91-11-4176-1620 • *Fax:* 91-11-4176-1630 • www.hayhouse.co.in

Distributed in Canada by: Raincoast Books,
2440 Viking Way, Richmond, B.C. V6V 1N2
Phone: 1-800-663-5714 • *Fax:* 1-800-565-3770 • www.raincoast.com

Take Your Soul on a Vacation

Visit www.HealYourLife.com® to regroup, recharge, and reconnect with your own magnificence. Featuring blogs, mind-body-spirit news, and life-changing wisdom from Louise Hay and friends.

Visit www.HealYourLife.com today!